ANELISSE

A True Story of Child Abuse

ADRIANA BELLINI

AUTHOR'S NOTE

Some names and identifying details have been changed to protect the privacy of individuals. In order to maintain their anonymity, in some instances I have changed some identifying characteristics and details such as physical properties, occupations, and places of residence. I have also purposely re-arranged the chronological order of some supporting events in order to maintain anonymity of persons involved.

Cover Photo By: Joel Funk

Monarch Publishing House
Publication Date: August 18, 2013
Copyright © 2013 Adriana Bellini
All rights reserved.
ISBN: **0615885063**
ISBN-13: **978-0615885063**

DEDICATION

This work is dedicated to those who have survived abuse, as well as those who were taken from this world too soon as a result.

~

This book is also dedicated to those whose acts of kindness and generosity allow me to be able to share my story today.

ADRIANA BELLINI

TABLE OF CONTENTS

PROLOGUE

As I tiptoe through the upstairs hall of our old farmhouse, I silently pray I don't wake my stepfather. A few steps down the cold hardwood floor I stop in front of my little brother's room when I see a faint trace of light. As I peek my head in, I see that he has built a small fort in the corner of his room made solely from his SpongeBob Squarepants comforter and many cleverly placed thumbtacks. Outside his fort, he has arranged his Army Man action figures in a straight line protecting the small entrance.

"What are you doing, David?" I whisper to him from the doorway. Poking his head through the entrance of the fort, he shines his flashlight directly into my eyes, momentarily blinding me. He looks at me with his big brown eyes, and begins opening his mouth to speak. Instead, he stops mid-sentence and puts his head down.

"What's wrong?" I ask, trying to blink away the white dots now floating across my vision.

"Nothing," he replies. I know that's not the truth.

I walk over to him and sit down on the floor outside of his fort. "You can tell me if something's wrong, David. I'm here if you need to talk."

"I want to go live with Mom-mom."

I'd like to go live with Mom-mom too, I think to myself. However, I know my mother would never allow anyone to raise her children for her, regardless what would be best for us.

Our grandmother, whom we call Mom-mom, is something of a second mother to us; possibly even the only good example of a mother we really have. She never fails to attend our school functions, read stories to us before bed when we stay over, and teach us valuable lessons like how to tie our shoes. She's also the first person our mother runs to whenever there is trouble, and in our family, there's always plenty.

"I know you love being at Mom-mom's house, and you will be there tomorrow after school. Go to sleep. The sooner you go to sleep, the sooner you'll be there." He smiles slightly, only partially consoled, and lays his head down on his pillow.

David loves his daily routine of taking the school bus to Mom-mom's after school; there, he feels safe and is treated well. My twin sister Maddie and I used to have the same routine until we got to high school and realized that even though spending time at Mom-mom's was a great temporary escape from the madness at our own home, it made going home that much more difficult.

"Yes, I'm going to Mom-mom's house tomorrow, and I'm never coming back here," he says with anger and sadness in his eyes.

I carefully reach inside the fort and lift my hand, gently brushing his eyelids closed with my fingertips as I had done nearly every night when he was an infant. He would fall asleep so easily that way in his bassinette; I hoped it would have the same effect this night. He snuggles further down into the heap of fluffy blankets inside his fort and prepares for sleep. I back out of his protective cave slowly and carefully, as not to tear it down or disturb the Army Men standing at attention outside, and leave him to his dream world.

As I pull his bedroom door closed, as softly and with as little noise as possible, I hear the faint sound of the wooden floor creaking down the hall. With my hand still holding on to the door handle, I hold my breath to listen for the source of the sound, barely able hear anything over the pounding of my own heart beating madly out of my chest.

I stand still as a statue feeling adrenaline racing through me, my knuckles white from the tight grip I wasn't aware I had on the doorknob. My body trembling and frozen with fear, I stand there waiting and listening. I hear someone getting out of bed.

Oh, shit. I should've just gone to bed and minded my own damned business.

I can feel my heart leaping into my throat and my stomach churn as my dinner does somersaults inside; I have woken my parents, and for this, I will surely pay.

ADRIANA BELLINI

CHAPTER ONE

My name is Anelisse Adams and at eighteen years old, I'm the eldest of three children. My sister Maddie, whose full name is Madelyn, is my twin. She prefers to be called 'Maddie' over 'Madelyn' because she thinks Madelyn sounds like an old lady's name; I think it's a beautiful name. Maddie and I are only separated in age by three minutes; however, it feels more like three years.

Though Maddie and I are twins, we are not identical; we're fraternal twins and we do not look alike; in fact, we barely look related. I take after my mother's Irish side of the family with my reddish-blond hair, blue eyes, fair skin, and light sprinkling of freckles across my nose while Maddie takes after our biological father's Hispanic side and has dark brown hair, hazel eyes, and an olive complexion.

Maddie is a feisty spirit who often defies societal norms for fun. An artist and fashion guru at heart, she's the one who gave me my nickname: Lissy. (Short story behind the nickname; she couldn't pronounce Anelisse when she was a baby and called me Lissy instead. It stuck.)

The youngest member of the household is my little brother David, whom I love more than anything else in the entire world. David is a chubby little boy with unruly brown hair and dark brown eyes and at eight years old, he's ten years younger than Maddie and I, which often results in my role as sister crossing over into "mother" quite frequently, a role I gladly take on for the sweet little cherub-faced boy who once literally saved my life.

Ed Adams is the head of our family and is quite well known in our small town of Arbor Falls for owning Adams' Farm, his family's produce farm, which has been a staple of the small New Jersey farm town for several generations. He is also well known around town for his time spent as a volunteer firefighter and as a daily patron to the local pub. Ed has many jobs, but seems most dedicated to his job as a functioning alcoholic.

Ed was a handsome man when he and my mother first met; Italian features of dark hair and tanned skin made his white teeth shine. Nearly all my friends had a crush on him when we were children; they thought he looked like John Stamos from the television show *Full House*. That was a long time ago, and since then years of hard labor and heavy drinking have drastically taken their toll on his appearance. Though presently only in his forties, he appears much older with his leathery skin darkened and dried out by many years of harvesting summer crops in the sun. His once-black hair has turned silvery along the front and sides of his face and has begun receding. Still, he is a handsome man in older age and the local divorcees love him.

Ed is David's biological father, though he officially

adopted Maddie and me at the age of four when he married our mother, Anna Kelly. Our mother is a physically beautiful woman with wavy chestnut hair, fair skin, and warm brown eyes. The years have taken a gentle toll on her face, mostly in the form of tired eyes and frown lines, but her beauty remains. From pictures I've seen of my mother in her youth, she was tall and slender with a gorgeous curvy figure, full bust, and an immaculate fashion sense. Although she has put on weight with age, her figure is still as attractive as ever; not that anyone could tell in the nursing scrubs she always wears.

My mother is of Irish-English descent and had a financially comfortable upbringing with all the latest in fashion and beauty. Fresh out of high school, my mother had dreams of owning a successful high-end salon and became a beauty stylist. She was so talented that she was being eyed to work for top names in the beauty industry like Chloe and Chanel, but she put her career on hold to start a family with my biological father. When their marriage didn't work out, my mother became a nurse in order to provide for two little girls on her own instead of resuming the path to her dream job in the beauty industry.

My mother is not a drinker or gambler, but she loves to read, smoke cigarettes, and drink coffee. She is a diabetic who refuses to accept the reality that she indeed has diabetes, despite the fact that she's a nurse and knows better than to eat a diet of Tastykakes and McDonald's because of the severe consequences on her health. I don't know much else about my mother as a person except that she loves cats, loves to read, and hates everyone; including Mom-mom, who is her mother.

Family members have told me that my mother used to

be a very fun, popular, friendly woman who loved to dance and lived for socializing. Apparently, her personality changed drastically from wild extrovert to insecure introvert after she met my father. Though I've never met my biological father, I have seen pictures of him and heard things about him from Mom-mom. My mother simply won't speak of him.

My biological father was (I've been told) a very handsome man of Puerto Rican descent. He and my mother fell madly in love very quickly. Unsurprisingly, as quickly as their love grew, just as quickly it died. They tried to make it work for the sake of Maddie and me, but when my mother caught him in bed with another woman, she left him forever. Still, the bitterness of that break-up seemed to stay with my mother for many years to follow.

After our mother left our father, she, Maddie, and I lived at Mom-mom's house temporarily while she went to school to become a nurse. Maddie and I loved living at our grandmother's house; it was a home full of love, toys, and yummy snacks. What more could any little girl need? If Maddie and I had it our way, we would've lived with Mom-mom until we were forty.

Our Mom-mom, Elizabeth (Betty, or Bette as my grandfather called her) Johnson may have provided the love of a traditional grandmother, but she certainly didn't look the part. She appeared very young for her age, which she claimed every year on her birthday was twenty-nine. With her wavy dark auburn hair styled perfectly, dark brown eyes with tiny gold flecks accentuated with black mascara and liquid liner, and a perfect size-six figure, she was a true fashionista and modeled herself after the gorgeous and elegant Elizabeth Taylor.

Mom-mom's house was impeccably decorated on the interior in antique French and Edwardian style designs in various shades of blue and gold. The home was a gorgeous colonial style with a grand foyer and large sweeping staircase adorned with a massive crystal chandelier. Mom-mom kept her home immaculately clean and people often commented about how you could quite literally eat off the floor. Mom-mom's home was her greatest possession and she took pride in keeping it clean, but considering the fervor with which she cleaned, it seemed to me more like compulsion that drove her, as opposed to pride.

Though Mom-mom's home was stunning and looked as if it were straight out of the pages of Better Homes & Gardens magazine, it was indeed a "home" in the true sense of the word, there were just certain rooms we were not allowed to step foot into, and others purposed specifically for us to make a mess in and play.

Our Pop-pop, Mom-mom's husband, had turned one of the bedrooms in the house into a playroom for us kids. In the playroom, we could hang our artwork, eat snacks, color, play dolls, and perform whatever activities we wanted to do. The backyard had a swing set, a child-sized kitchen set, and a plastic playhouse in which we only played twice because spiders tended to weave ornate webs inside. One of the best places to play in her house was the garage; this was Maddie's favorite place to play because in there we were allowed to draw on the walls. Maddie is quite the artist and over the years has covered the walls with her work.

What made Mom-mom's house so much like a real home was that Mom-mom was very loving and gave us plenty of love and affection. She always fed us breakfast, lunch, and dinner, and would read stories to us at night.

Mom-mom and allowed us to just be children. Sometimes at night, we'd lie in her huge bed with her and she'd light a cigarette and spell out words in the dark room with the lit end. Maddie and I would say the letters as she wrote them and shout out the answers when she was done. Words like "love" and "pretty" and "smile" put us in a loving, peaceful state of mind as we fell asleep. Maddie and I both felt so safe and happy living at Mom-mom's; to us, it was like being part of a fairy tale family.

Mom-mom was married to a man named Jack Johnson, who was my mother's stepfather. We knew him as Pop-pop and he'd been married to our grandmother long before we were born. Pop-pop was in the Army Air Corps as a younger man and had been a POW, or Prisoner of War, in Germany for fourteen months during World War II. He had a Purple Heart, Prisoner of War, and many other medals that Maddie always asked to look at. He was fun and he adored Mom-mom with all his heart. A big fan of western movies and every Philadelphia sports team, he taught me to read at the age of four by reading the Sports section of the newspaper to me during my many hours in his lap.

Life was perfect and happy for Maddie and me at Mom-mom's house; however, my mother desired to have her own home with a husband and her children, a need I did not understand at a young age, but can understand now, despite the fact that living with Mom-mom was the only real home-like experience I would ever have.

CHAPTER TWO

I still remember when my mother brought Ed home to Mom-mom's house to meet us for the first time. We were about four years old and quite a handful. Mom-mom was busy bathing Maddie and me when my mother came upstairs announcing she had someone she wanted us to meet. Mom-mom dried us off, put on our pajamas, and prepared us for our meeting with this new friend of our mother's.

"Your name is Ed?" I asked. "That's a stupid name."

"That's not a very nice thing to say now is it, Lissy? Apologize to the nice man and remember your manners." Mom-mom was big on the whole "manners" thing and always corrected our socially unacceptable behavior. To this day, people still comment regarding how well-mannered I am, so her efforts were certainly not in vain.

"I'm sorry, Ed. I didn't mean to be rude; I just thought Ed was a horse's name."

Ed looked at me with an immense warm smile and said, "It's ok, Kiddo. Ed *is* a horse's name!" He proceeded to sing the theme song to the vintage television show Mr. Ed. "I am Mr. Ed!"

I giggled heartily and decided that maybe he was a nice person. He liked Mr. Ed, so he must have some kind of fun side to him. I supposed we could probably be friends.

Maddie took to him immediately and thought the world of him. He became one of our favorite people to hang out with because he had no trouble sitting cross-legged on the playroom floor with us dressing Barbies and letting us paint his face with make-up. He also let us watch scary movies and brought us McDonald's Happy Meals every time he took our mother out on a date.

One evening, after several months of dating, Ed and my mother arrived at Mom-mom's house early from a romantic outing and announced that they were getting married.

"Oh, that's wonderful! Congratulations you two." Mom-mom said, giving huge hugs and kisses to both of them. Nothing made Mom-mom happier than her daughter finally finding a husband.

"Congratulations," said Pop-pop, shaking Ed's hand in ultra-manly fashion, "take care of those girls, you hear?"

"Yes, sir." Ed said smiling.

"So, when's the wedding?" Mom-mom asked.

"Well," said my mother hesitantly, "we've decided to elope." She covered her head with her arms to protect it from the smack she expected to get from her mother.

"Elope?!" Mom-mom looked as if my mother had admitted to wearing white shoes after Labor Day, an awful fashion faux pas that would've made my grandmother faint in horror.

"Don't kill me! We made the decision *together* to spend the money we would have spent on a wedding on a home for the girls and ourselves. Surprise again!" My mother was beaming with joy.

To that, Mom-mom and my mother began hugging each other and crying. Pop-pop and Ed began talking about the house while Maddie and I stood there watching.

"Wait, so we're moving?" Maddie asked, interrupting the cheerful banter coming from the adults. I wasn't quite sure whether she was about to burst out in cheer or burst out in tears.

Everyone froze as if just realizing Maddie and I were present.

My mother bent down to look Maddie in the eyes and said with a smile, "Yes, Maddie, we're moving, to our very own home!"

Maddie carefully processed the idea in her head, and then exclaimed, "Hooray!"

Everyone shared in a sigh of relief.

"Can I get a dog?" Maddie asked, excited.

"Ha! Your mother and I will have to have a talk about that first, kiddo." Ed said, affectionately tussling her hair.

Mom-mom and Pop-pop were very happy our mother had found a man to treat her well, and even more so that the man she found would be a wonderful father to Maddie and me. They hugged and congratulated us all one last time, then left us to continue the conversation in privacy.

After breaking the abundance of surprising news, my

mother and Ed spoke with us and explained to Maddie and me that we were becoming a family and that Ed had bought us a house to live in near his family's farm. The farmhouse we were moving to sat on over twenty acres of land and had once been owned and occupied by his Uncle Vince, Aunt Grace, and their two sons. They made sure to stress the fact that the house was only a short distance away from Mom-mom and Pop-pop's house, a detail that was very important to Maddie and me because we loved our grandparents dearly.

"So the house is close by?" I asked.

"Yes, it's only a five minute drive from here." Ed assured me.

"Does anyone live there now?"

"No." Ed said, looking like he knew exactly where the conversation was heading.

"Can we go see it?" I asked hopefully.

Maddie and I looked at each other, then back at Ed.

"PLEASE!?" We pleaded in unison.

Laughing at our shameless display of beggary, Ed happily agreed to take us over to have a look at the vacant house.

CHAPTER THREE

On the drive to see our new home, Maddie and I squirmed in our seats; we could barely contain our excitement. I dreamed of having our own backyard to plant flowers, maybe have a swing set or a pool, or maybe even a pet of my own! There were endless possibilities! Maybe I would have my own room with a pink princess bed with a white headboard and soft fluffy carpet and a cat named Fluffy who would be soft and white and sleep in my bed with me at night. I was ecstatic and Ed couldn't drive fast enough for me.

As we drove down the road and made a turn onto a country road, or back road as we call them here in Jersey, I saw a fenced-in creek sitting on open land of about ten acres but no houses. For a moment, I thought we had gone the wrong way.

"Are we lost, Ed?" I couldn't see anything from the road other than what looked like growing corn stalks on part of the land. A dense wall of trees surrounded the large piece of land around its large perimeter.

"Nope, we're here. The house is just around this bend." He pointed with his head to his left and I saw a mailbox. The butterflies in my stomach were flapping their wings wildly.

"I see it! Look Maddie- a mailbox! That's our own mailbox for our own house and our own mail! I'm going to get lots of letters," I bragged, and then practically dragged Maddie right out of her car seat trying to pull her closer to the window. I wanted her to see her mailbox too.

We pulled into a driveway nearly hidden by overgrown grass and stepped out of Ed's truck onto the crunchy gravel. All I could see were trees, which made me wonder if the house really existed, but then Ed began walking toward a dirt path heading into the trees so we began to follow him.

As we headed into the wooded area, I heard nothing but wind, birds chirping, and the sound of our footsteps in the dirt. The sun was setting, casting a soothing glow on the leaves of the trees along the path. Ed stopped in front of a rusty wrought-iron gate and looked back at us.

"Are you ready to see your new home?"

"YES!" I wasn't even attempting to hide my excitement. Maddie was squirming around in my mother's arms fussing a bit. It was getting late and she was tired.

"Go." Was all Maddie could muster, and then she dove her face into my mother's neck and squeezed her tight.

Ed opened the gate, which was a bit difficult due to the overgrowth of lawn and bushes that had been neglected while the house sat vacant. He stomped down some especially tall grass with his boots and ushered us through the gate. Once through the gate, I stopped to savor the image of the large old farmhouse all alone in the middle of a large piece of land with tall, luscious evergreen trees around the perimeter that stood higher than the house itself. It was as if we had our own private piece of the town secretly hidden in the woods behind the farm.

We finally had our own home, and it was perfect. It was a home in which we could throw huge holiday dinner parties, make new family memories, and have big birthday parties and pets and… My thoughts stopped abruptly as I was interrupted by the sudden realization that we did not have neighbors.

"How come we don't have any neighbors?" It was a bit unusual for me to live in a secluded place, as Mom-mom's house was in a community with other homes, and prior to living at Mom-mom's, my mother, Maddie, and I had lived in an apartment building containing many small units. Most of the tenants had been families with children about our age that Maddie and I could play with.

"As you know, Lissy, I'm a farmer and farmers need land to grow lots of crops on, which is why we need to have so much land. Farming is my job and I do it every day at the break of dawn, and since we have a house on the very same land I will be working on, it's very convenient. Also, tractors are very loud, which can disturb neighbors, so it's best to be in a place where my farming sounds won't disturb other people."

Ed was very good with words and explaining things to me. I liked to understand the reasoning behind everything and Ed seemed to get that about me. I thought more about the advantages of the privacy I'd have without neighbors and daydreamed of dancing between cornstalks unseen by the world. I smiled. Maybe it could be a cool thing after all.

Surveying the state of my new old home, I noticed that the tall three-story farmhouse appeared to be a bit unstable in its stance and moderately worn from neglect; the wraparound porch was missing some rungs in its railings and shabby layers of paint peeled away to reveal the naked wood beneath. The bushes and flowers had once been lovingly planted in a formation that would have beautifully accented the porch today if they were still living. Weathered gray wooden siding hung onto the home looking hopeless and wary; it seemed to me like the house had been extremely lonely without owners.

You poor house. I thought to myself. *We need to bring you back to life. Don't worry; we'll get you fixed up in no time!* I regularly felt empathy for inanimate objects. Though I'm sure that empathy is just projection of my own fears of being abandoned, neglected, and forgotten, I can't help but feel sadness for any lone object, animal, shoe, person, etc.

Looking up, an oval window in what looked to be the attic caught my eye. It was one of those creepy windows you always see in scary movies where you'd expect to see a ghostly figure suddenly appear. I stared a little longer at the window to make sure nobody was going to appear. If the house was haunted, I was staying at Mom-mom's. After staring long enough to be convinced the house was paranormally sound and ghost-free, I decided to go in the house and join my family, who had already made their way inside.

As I entered the home for the first time, I suspected that the house had been sitting vacant for quite a while. Walking through the living room after closing the front door, I felt cobwebs grabbing on to my face.

Naturally, I thought, *three people walk in ahead of me and I'm the one who walks directly into the webs.* Peeling away the silky strands of web, I hoped a spider hadn't landed somewhere on me. I shuddered at the thought; I hated spiders.

Boxes covered in dust littered the living room. It seemed Ed's family had left behind some of their belongings. Peeking inside one box, I saw games and toys that had obviously belonged to Ed's cousins. Most of the toys I had never seen before, as they had been produced around the 1950s, well before my generation. Closing the box lid carefully, as not to damage any of the vintage and possibly sentimental items, I decided to explore the rest of the house.

Immediately upon entering the bathroom, I noticed how unusually large it was.

"Wow, this bathroom is humongous!" I thought it was fit for a queen with the huge tub and ample floor space.

"It's a handicap accessible bathroom." Ed informed me, "My Uncle built this house for his two sons who were disabled. You'll notice around the house that the doorways are wide and there are wheelchair ramps instead of steps, except for the stairs leading to the second floor. My cousins had everything they needed on the first floor." Ed took me around the house and showed me all the handicap features that had been built into the home, and then we joined my mother and Maddie in the kitchen.

"So girls, what do you think?" My mother asked.

"We love it!" Maddie said. "But why are all the mirrors

turned around and on the ground? That's freaky!"

My mother laughed. Maddie, the queen of horror movies, was obviously scared by that odd occurrence. "Ed's family is Italian. They're superstitious and they believe that when someone dies in the house, you must cover all of the mirrors so that the soul of the person doesn't get trapped in the mirror."

"What? Someone died in this house?" Maddie's eyes were as wide as saucers and her mouth was hanging open in shock. I couldn't believe our mother would expect us to live in a house where someone died.

My mother explained, "Yes, Ed's cousins both passed away here at home from a rare genetic illness. Their mother Grace passed away in this house shortly after. Don't be scared; they're our family and they died of natural causes."

"Well I'm glad they weren't all slaughtered here," Maddie said, "But it's still creepy."

I had to agree; it was creepy, but they were family and they died peacefully. If I were to see their ghosts, I'd just say hello and thank them for letting us have this house. I don't necessarily believe in ghosts, but I'm not going to say it's impossible for them to be real. I don't want a ghost to come to me in the middle of the night and scare the crap out of me to prove to me that they exist; no way, no thanks.

My mother convinced us not to worry about the deaths that occurred in the house and to focus on the home's positive attributes. Even though the house was old and in need of some TLC, it had great potential. Its large rooms were perfect for my mother's country decorating style and the hardwood floors, once sanded and polished, would be perfect for skating on in my socks. The ceilings were high and the bedrooms were large enough for me to do cartwheels with ease (I know, I tested them myself). Ed promised we could move in just as soon as he set up the gas and electric; then, he'd begin the repairs. I couldn't wait!

Heading back to Mom-mom's for the night, I dozed off on Maddie's shoulder in the back of Ed's truck dreaming of all the fun we'd have in our new home; our creepy, awesome, scary, secluded, big home... and tried extremely hard not to think about dead people possibly haunting the house.

CHAPTER FOUR

Once we were all moved in, we got busy settling into our new role as a complete family. Maddie and I had our last names changed from our biological father's name, Feliciano, to the name of our new adoptive father, Adams. Everything was new; new family, new home, new father, new name... I was happy to feel like I belonged somewhere and felt hopeful that we would all have a great life and be one big happy family just like in the movies.

Maddie and I began attending kindergarten that first September in the new house. My mother was working a lot at the nursing home where she'd been working on the evening shift after graduating nursing school. We didn't see her very often except on her days off considering that she left for her shift in the early afternoon and arrived home well after we had gone to bed.

Ed was with us the majority of the time on a daily basis that fall. Winter was coming and work on the farm was slow since it only operated as a business from mid-spring until October 31st, Halloween. The off-season enabled him to have lots of free time to spend with Maddie and me.

That first winter in our new home was a time of adjustment; we were all finding our footing in our new place in a unified family. We planned game nights, had Sunday dinners, and got to know each other better. We also fought a lot over matters of discipline, especially Ed and me. It was difficult for me as a child to adjust to having this new person in my life taking on a role as an authority figure. I never had a father (that I could remember) and I didn't really understand why I needed one now. Mom-mom, Pop-pop, and my mother were really my family and I listened to them when they told me to do something because I loved them and wanted to do what I was supposed to do to make them happy.

I had trouble respecting Ed's authority when it came to him telling me to do practically anything. Ed had a way of ordering me to do something instead of asking me to do it. I didn't feel he treated me with respect, so I became defiant against him.

I am, to this day, a person who responds to requests that are phrased in a way that make me feel as though I'm doing something to help another person. I'm a people-pleaser; if you're good to me and ask me for help, I'll do anything for you. If you order me around and take away my choice, you will be met with resistance.

Maddie listened to everyone and always did what she was told. She was a good girl and didn't like to get in trouble; not that I enjoyed being punished; I just didn't necessarily care to listen to Ed. I had no respect for him because his moods changed so drastically and frequently. All my young mind knew was that he acted quite mean sometimes for the oddest reasons and I couldn't quite figure out why.

CHAPTER FIVE

After our first fall and winter in the new home, spring came along and Ed had plenty of work to do on the farm. Because my mother worked in the evenings and Ed worked until around nine o'clock every evening, we began going to Mom-mom's house every day after school until Ed's work on the farm was done.

Afterward, he'd come pick us up in his big blue truck and take us home and put us to bed. That was our daily routine on the days my mother worked and Maddie and I enjoyed the opportunity to spend more time with Mom-mom and Pop-pop, our two most favorite people in the entire world, aside from our mother. As a nurse, my mother had every other weekend off and those days we would all work on the farm as a family and pick peaches or peppers or hunt for ripe watermelon, which is actually a fun pastime when you're a young child, though that's not so much the case when one becomes an adolescent.

When summer vacation came, Maddie and I spent nearly every day out in the fields on the farm hitching rides on the back of Ed's tractor, picking peaches, dancing between the cornstalks, and singing loudly along to our portable CD players (quite badly, I might add) until we were tired out. We had a blast and Ed cooked out on the barbecue out back of our house almost every day. His firefighter friends came over quite often too; they were nice to Maddie and me and let us have soda. My mom didn't allow us to have soda in the house, so for us that was a real treat!

My mom worked a lot that summer and we missed her a great deal. Sometimes Ed would let us stay up until she got home so we could play rummy and eat snacks or watch a movie together. Maddie and I could never stay awake through an entire movie, but we were content just to be sleeping near our mother whom we didn't get to see very often.

As the summer drew on, Ed seemed to spend more time hanging out with his friends out back than spending any time with us. He began acting strange; sometimes he'd be angry and snarky for no apparent reason, or display a very nice, charming side of himself who liked to laugh at his own jokes and refer to me as "Kiddo." I came to learn that this "nice guy" was drunk Ed, while the mean version of Ed meant he had drunk enough beers to quench an army. Sober Ed was calm, fun, and a good guy, and we were seeing less and less of him as the days passed.

When the back-to-school sales began and the time came to buy school clothes and supplies for our first grade classes, we resumed our after-school routine at Mom-mom's house. As he did the previous school year, Ed would pick us up from her house at the end of his workday on the farm.

One night while Maddie and I were getting our

backpacks ready for Ed to come get us, Mom-mom came into the playroom with a surprise.

"Guess what, girls? We're going to have a sleepover tonight! Now go get your pajamas on and I'll get out your sleeping bags. You girls can have a campout in the playroom." Her excitement seemed forced, which worried me.

"On a school night?" I found that quite odd.

"Yes, but just this once. Ed had to… work late."

I could tell by the look on her usually sunny face that she not only just made that up on the spot, but that she was also struggling to convince us that Ed had indeed had to work late that night. I decided to accept her explanation despite the fact that I didn't believe it.

We camped out in the playroom after Mom-mom read us a story. That night, while listening to Maddie breathing heavily as she slept hanging half out of her sleeping bag, I lied awake wondering what could possibly be the real reason for this impromptu slumber party and I hoped everything was going to be ok

CHAPTER SIX

The next morning our mother came over to our grandmother's house to pick us up for school; she looked tired and disheveled. A sad look in her eyes made me want to hug her, but I decided against it when the look of sadness suddenly switched to a look of madness.

"Go wait in the car, you two. I'll be there in a minute. I have to talk to Mom-mom." She was very angry. Was she mad at us? Did we do something wrong? I had no clue what was going on, but I started trying to guess what I may have done to cause her anger.

By the look on Maddie's face, I could tell she was doing the exact same thing. "Come on, Maddie," I said softly, "Mommy wants us to get in the car, so let's go." Maddie was hurt by my mother's tone of voice. I was certain she'd never snapped at us like that before; we weren't quite sure how to react to her mood.

"We did something wrong." Maddie worried aloud as she followed me to the car.

"We don't know what's wrong yet, so let's just get in the

car and wait to see what Mommy says."

I opened the rear driver's side door of my mom's burgundy SUV, tossed our backpacks in, and climbed in; Maddie followed. We waited for what seemed like forever but was probably only a few minutes when our mother came storming out of Mom-mom's house, slamming the front door behind her. She charged over to the car, ripped the door open, plopped down in the driver's seat, and slammed the door shut with intense force.

"What's wrong, Mommy? What happened with Ed last night? Why are you mad at Mom-mom? Are you mad at us?" Though a barrage of questions might not have been the best idea at that particular point in time, I couldn't stop the words from tumbling out of my mouth.

"Shut up!" My mother shouted angrily. "Everything is all messed up and you two make everything ten times more difficult with all your questions."

"What did we do?" I could feel my eyes stinging as the tears were forming. I looked over at Maddie, whose face was red. She gave me a look that told me she wondered the same thing.

Our mother covered her face with her hands and released a frustrated muffled shout. Clearly, she was extremely upset by whatever it was. After a moment of cooling down, she opened her visor to check her face in the mirror. She wiped away some smeared black eyeliner and stared at herself for a moment, then took a deep breath in, held it, and let it out very slowly.

She turned herself around to face us in the back seat. Then she said with sweetness and a sudden smile, "Ok girls, that's enough of that. How about McDonald's for breakfast? Who wants hot cakes? I do!" Suddenly, everything that just happened didn't.

*   *   *   *   *

After school that day, everything was back to normal despite the fact that Maddie and I hadn't gotten any real explanation for what had happened the night before from either our mother or our grandmother, and I wasn't optimistic that we were going to get one any time soon. Perhaps I hadn't done anything wrong after all. Though I felt some relief at the thought of not being the cause of the trouble, I still worried what could have possibly made my mother act so uncharacteristically mean to us.

We went to Mom-mom's as usual after school. While I helped Maddie with her homework at the kitchen table, Pop-pop made us a dinner of London broil with mushrooms, with steamed carrots and baked potatoes, his favorite meal.

Distracted from helping Maddie by the savory aroma of the meal being prepared, I wondered what kind of meat London broil was. I asked Maddie if she knew.

"It's black chicken," she informed me with a serious tone.

I heard Pop-pop stifling a laugh and pretending to look at the "black chicken" in the oven.

Maddie screwed up her face in defense of being laughed at. "What's so funny, Pop-pop?" She crossed her arms and sat back in her chair quite roughly.

He walked over to her with oven mitts still on his hands. "I'm not laughing at you; I'm laughing because of you! You're hilarious! I think you've come up with a very imaginative and creative explanation of what London broil is." He laughed and gave Maddie a sort of awkward headlock hug over the back of her chair. "London Broil is steak. It's beef and beef comes from a cow. 'Black chicken.' Ha! You just made my day, Maddie." He chuckled again and resumed tending to his culinary creation.

I looked over at Maddie, who had tried to remain appearing stern and offended but couldn't help but crack a smile at Pop-pop's reaction to her misinformed remark. She giggled, "It seemed like the right answer, so I said it."

I burst out in laughter. "I believed you! You really sounded like you knew what you were saying! Ha-ha!" We laughed until our stomachs ached, then settled down when Pop-pop put dinner on the table. Mom-mom joined us for the meal and in no time we were all laughing together yet again about Maddie's black chicken. Ten years later, we still tease her about it whenever any of us cooks or orders steak.

The rest of the week passed with no more talk of the events that had occurred the night of our sleepover at Mom-mom's, but the weekend that followed would tell us more than any child should ever learn.

CHAPTER SEVEN

When the weekend arrived, Maddie and I were happy that my mother had off from work. We had finished all of our homework Friday night so we'd have free time to play on Saturday and Sunday. Unfortunately, rain ruined our outdoor plans Saturday evening, so my mother, Ed, Maddie, and I decided to watch a scary movie and make some marshmallow crispy rice treats.

As my mother stood over the stove melting together butter and marshmallows for our treats, Ed's emergency pager went off, beeping loudly in a series of tones that made no sense to me, but meant something to Ed. He walked over to the emergency radio he used specifically for his job at the fire company.

"Station 722, station 724, station 729, Arbor Falls, NJ. House fire..." said the dispatcher over the radio. We had come to learn that station 729 was Ed's station, and when that number was called, he had to go immediately to put out a fire.

"I'll be back as soon as possible," Ed told my mother,

who looked at him with a pained expression to which he took no notice and walked out the front door. Maddie and I remained silent during the tension-filled exchange. Noticing my mother's negative reaction in response to Ed having to run out, I wondered if Ed's firefighting duties had prevented him from being able to pick us up the other night; but if that was the case, why all the secrecy and anger over that? I thought that maybe my mother was being too sensitive.

"Should we wait for Ed to get back to watch the movie?" I asked. I wasn't sure of the general amount of time it took to extinguish a fire.

"No, that's ok, Lissy. We can go ahead and start the movie. Ed has seen it several times; it's one of his favorites," my mother said as she blended the crispy rice cereal with the melted marshmallow mixture. She seemed to have let her annoyance at Ed having to leave abruptly pass.

The movie we had chosen to watch that evening was entitled 'It', based on a book written by Stephen King, our mother's favorite author. Anna Adams was a dedicated fan of the author and owned every single book ever written by him, as well as every film version of his books. This was surely the reason Maddie became such a huge horror movie junkie; our mother had begun letting us watch Stephen King movies as soon as we were old enough to pay attention to the TV. Maddie had been obsessed with horror films ever since she first saw the movie *Pet Sematary*. Tonight's film, *It*, was in her list of top ten best horror movies of all time and she was getting impatient while waiting for us all to be ready.

"Come on, guys!" Maddie whined. "I have been waiting for you for like ever!"

Our mother finished up with the treats and set them on the counter to rest, and then we all sat down to watch the movie. While our mother settled down in her La-Z-Boy recliner with a cup of coffee and a cigarette, Maddie and I snuggled up together beneath our favorite blanket, which we called the cat blanket because it was patterned with a grey cat face on a white background. The blanket was something of a shared security blanket for Maddie and me. We fought over it constantly and kicked each other many times under the covers when one of us had more of the blanket than the other.

We watched the movie, which I found terribly horrifying since it was about a murderous clown who preyed on children; I think so, anyway. I'm not exactly sure. Because I had a serious unprovoked phobia of clowns since I was born, I had a habit of covering my eyes during scary movies and watched the entire movie through the tiniest slit of space between my fingers. Doing so made it much less scary for me to watch any horror movie, but also made me miss some important plot points.

As the movie ended and we polished off the remainder of our marshmallow treats, Ed arrived home. He nearly fell through the front door and was soaked from head to toe from the pouring rain outside. His face was streaked with black soot from the fire that had run down his face from the rain as mascara does when a wearer cries. He looked as if he were crying black tears and smelled like a raging bonfire and a curious pungent odor I later learned to recognize as beer. My mother shot up from her chair and confronted him immediately.

"Were you down at that firehouse drinking again?" she asked, "Are you drunk?" Her eyes were wild with anger.

"What? I am NOT drunk. You're crazy!" His denial was so emphatic that it emphasized his drunkenness instead of being convincing of his sobriety.

My mother was furious and looked as if her eyes were going to pop out of her head. "Get the fuck out! I am not crazy, you fucking piece of shit! I hate you and you do this shit in front of my daughters? Get the fuck out. Get the fuck OUT!"

Maddie and I huddled together holding hands on the couch watching them scream at each other; for me, this was scarier than the movie we had just seen. My mother forcefully shoved Ed toward the door and repeatedly told him to leave.

Maddie began to cry, "STOP! STOP! Mommy, please STOP!" She squeezed my hand tighter and tighter with each word she shouted.

"Yeah, stop Anna, you're scaring the little kiddos," Ed mocked. "Whiney whiney babies!"

Was he serious? Was he really mocking Maddie? It felt so surreal that he would treat Maddie like that in a moment where she was so obviously scared by two adults acting like lunatics.

"Seriously? You're making fun of my kid. YOU FUCKING SON OF A BITCH!" My mother was standing near a tall bookcase full of hardcover encyclopedias. She grabbed the first volume she could get her hands on and thrust it with all her might in Ed's direction. She missed. The book sailed past Ed's head into the wall and then fell to the floor with a thud.

For a moment, it seemed as if time slowed down almost

to a halt as I watched Ed's face twist up into a wild hate-filled look of sheer evil. His lips were tight and the corners of his mouth turned down hard. His nostrils flared and he was breathing heavily and quickly through them. Then, almost as if someone pressed fast forward, he flew toward my mother and slammed her bodily into the bookcase. He held her there by her neck and though I couldn't see his face, hers held a look of sheer terror and shock.

"You fucking cunt!" He spit in her face and proceeded to name-call. "You're a fucking whore. Everyone knows you fucked Jim Baker and everybody thinks you're a whore!" He swung hard and hit her directly in the side of her left cheek. I watched her body fall hard to the floor. She tried to say something, but I couldn't make it out. Ed hovered over her spewing profanities and insults while she lay there moaning.

I couldn't breathe. My stomach gurgled in pain and my whole body was shaking. My mouth was as dry as the desert and my heart was pounding out of my chest. Maddie was crying hysterically and practically pulling my whole arm off while attempting to cover herself with the cat blanket.

I have no idea what came over me in that instant, but something in my nearly four-foot tall, six-year-old petite frame told me I could take on this six-foot tall grown man. I flew off the couch and began punching and kicking him with all my might.

"Get off my mommy! Get out of here! You're mean and nobody-". As I was screaming my hatred toward him and hitting him as hard as I could, a sudden searing pain in my head forced me to halt mid-motion. My head snapped back but my body flew forward; Ed had grabbed me by the hair and yanked me off him onto the floor.

Still hanging onto me by gripping a handful of my hair, he put his face so close to mine our noses almost touched. "You can't beat me, kiddo. I'm much bigger than you." The stale scent of beer on his breath as he bragged made me sick. I could feel chunks rising in my throat. Yanking hard on my hair one last time to prove his point that he could beat me, Ed pushed me onto the couch back next to Maddie, who was frozen in place with fear. My scalp stung, neck ached, and I felt nauseous.

"Mommy, my stomach hurts," I said, feeling as if I had run 10 miles. I wasn't sure I could hold back the vomit.

"That's because you've got the devil in you." Ed glared at me. I hugged Maddie tight, wondering if I really had the devil inside of me. Tears began streaming down my face as if my tear ducts had suddenly just remembered to react to the situation. This angered Ed, and he came lunging toward the couch.

He's going to kill us, I thought.

I began to pray. We didn't go to church but believed in God so I didn't really know what to pray for when death was imminent, so I closed my eyes and began reciting my goodnight prayer aloud while holding Maddie's hand.

"Now I lay me down to sleep, I pray the Lord my soul to keep, if I should die before I wake-". Maddie began reciting the prayer with me.

Behind him, my mother yelled out, "You fucking pussy, beating up girls!"

Just as he was about to turn around, she quickly raised a

cast iron pan she had hung on the wall for decoration and hit him square in the head. I felt only a little bit guilty for experiencing a feeling of happiness as he hit the ground.

CHAPTER EIGHT

As Ed was lying on the floor unconscious from the blow to his head, my mother felt for his pulse; thankfully, he had one. As quickly as she could, she grabbed me and Maddie (who was clutching the cat blanket for dear life), her keys and her purse, and ran out the front door to her SUV. She motioned to us to grab her purse from her as she fumbled with her keys. We heard the electronic locks release in the night silence and quickly opened the car doors and jumped in.

With tears in her eyes, my mother drove away from the farmhouse as fast as she could. When we reached the main road off the farm, I realized I had been holding my breath. I exhaled a long, deep sigh and a sudden and urgent need to sleep washed over me. I turned to Maddie, who was shedding silent tears and rubbing her face with the cat blanket, and gave her a huge hug.

"Are you ok, Maddie?" It broke my heart to see her sad.

"He is a mean person and I never want to go back there. He hit Mommy and pulled your hair out. I wish we never met him." She snuggled further down into the blanket and offered me some of it. We had no idea where our mother was taking us, nor did we care as long as it was far, far away from that evil man. As we both dozed off under the cat blanket in the back of the truck, my mother kept on driving.

*   *   *   *   *

When I next awoke, we were parked outside Mom-mom's house. The car was still running, but my mother was no longer in it. I assumed she went in to talk to Mom-mom and I hoped we were going to stay there for the night.

Maddie was still asleep next to me, her mouth hanging wide open. She still had her seatbelt on but had pulled her legs up through the belt to her chest, hugged her legs, and was leaning her head on the door. She looked like her neck would hurt if she stayed in that position much longer. I gently shook her awake and moved further away from her to give her some more space.

"Take your seatbelt off and lie down, Maddie." I patted the seat between us. Her eyes glazed over, she said nothing, but removed her seatbelt and stretched out into the extra space. I gave her the entire cat blanket and she went right back to sleep.

This feels like a bad Lifetime Movie. I thought. *This can't really be our life.*

Everything felt so surreal. I wasn't sure what was going to happen next, but my stomach was in knots with anxiety.

Something like this probably happened when we had to sleep at Mom-mom's the other night. What if she goes back to him after this? My stomach turned at the thought.

I felt extremely fearful that my mother was going to forgive Ed and take him back. If, in fact, this had happened before and she took him back, wouldn't that mean she would do it again?

Staring at Mom-mom's front door, I wondered if I should go inside, but I didn't want to leave Maddie alone in the car. For a moment, I considered beeping the horn to get my mom's attention, but not only would that wake Maddie up and make my mother extremely upset with me, it would also disturb Mom-mom's neighbors.

I decided to just sit and wait. I leaned my head against the glass window of the car door; it felt cool and soothing against my throbbing head. Remembering that Maddie had said Ed pulled *out* my hair, and not only pulled, I wondered if I had a bald spot. I felt the back of my head where he had pulled from, but I couldn't really tell how much hair was gone. It hurt like crazy to touch it. The skin was tender and though I wasn't exactly able to feel a bald spot, I worried what it looked like.

Just then, my mom came walking up to the car. Quietly opening the car door, she motioned to me to come on in the house. Nodding in Maddie's direction, my mother pointed at herself, a message I took to mean she would get Maddie out of the car. I grabbed our bags and my mom's purse and headed inside while my mother gently wrapped Maddie in the cat blanket and put her in her arms.

Mom-mom greeted me at the door with a somber face. From my hands she took the things I was carrying and placed them down next to us and picked me up to give me a huge hug.

"I'm so sorry you had to go through that, baby. Go on

in the kitchen; Pop-pop has some snacks waiting for you two. Your mother and I are going to go upstairs to my room and talk for a little bit." She kissed me on the forehead and put her hand on my back, gently nudging me in the direction of the kitchen.

In the kitchen, I found Pop-pop setting out dessert plates holding fresh slices of Entenmann's Crumb Coffee Cake.

"Hey Pops! Excited to see him, I ran over and flung my arms around his waist.

"Hey, doll!" Hugging me with one hand and holding a plate of cake in the other, he playfully pushed me over to the table. "Can you pour a glass of milk without spilling it?" he teased.

"Pop-pop I am not a baby. Of course I won't spill it!" Giggling as I carefully poured milk into the cups he set out, I feigned offense to his taunt. If anyone knew what a capable little girl I was, it was my Pop-pop.

Maddie came into the kitchen looking annoyed at being woken up; though when she caught sight of the Entenmann's cake on the table, her face lit up. "Hooray! Crumb cake! It's my favorite!" She licked her lips dramatically and sat down at the table. After I placed the milk neatly back in the fridge, I joined her, then Pop-pop grabbed some napkins and utensils and sat down too.

As we were enjoying our yummy treat, Pop-pop questioned us about the events of the evening. "So, do you girls want to tell me what happened tonight?"

Maddie, mouth full of cake and covered in powdered sugar and cinnamon, blurted out, "Ed choked Mommy and then hit her, and he pulled Lissy's hair out." As she spoke, crumbs flew out of her mouth.

"Ed said Lissy has the devil in her, probably because she tried to kick his butt." She stopped to take a drink of milk, her favorite drink aside from a local beverage known as 'Tak-a-Boost.'

After gulping nearly her entire glass in one shot, she continued her story, "Mommy hit him in the head with a pan, and he fell asleep. I thought maybe he was dead but Mommy checked his wrist and we found out he was just sleeping. He was on the floor snoring, and then we left and came here. I don't want to go back there. Can we stay here forever? Do you have any scary movies we can watch? Can I have more milk?"

I was shocked at the ease with which Maddie spoke of the situation. Either she was handling all of the madness of the evening extremely well, or she was a master at blocking it all out and moving on; I wasn't sure, but I was impressed. Either way, I was glad she wasn't crying anymore and was enjoying her dessert.

Pop-pop looked as though he was ready to hop in his car, drive to our home, and finish Ed off. Instead, he looked at me with pain in his eyes and asked me if I had anything to say about the situation.

"Well, Pops, it was really scary. I thought he was going to kill us, so I'm mostly feeling glad we're alive. I'm afraid of going back there. I'm scared of Ed; he was acting really crazy and I don't want to be hurt again."

Going over the scene in my head, I remembered one thing that was haunting me. I hesitated to share it with Pop-pop. I didn't want him to think I was foolish for my thoughts.

"Ed said I had the devil in me. Do you think I do? Is that possible? Could I have the devil in me and not even know it?"

Pop-pop looked concerned. "Well, Doll, that all depends on what you believe. That's a big question and it involves religion, something you girls weren't really brought up following."

Carefully considering how to word his response, he paused. After a long moment, he continued.

"In order for you to believe that you have the devil in you, you have to believe there is a devil. I personally believe in God and the devil, and I know you do not have the devil in you. There's no way any person, even if they believe the devil exists, could think that of you."

I felt like I had the devil in me and believed it to be possible to have the devil inside you without knowing it. I thought Pop-pop was just a bit biased.

Maybe he just can't see it because he loves me so much, I thought.

He noticed the doubtful look on my face. "Sometimes people say things they don't mean when they're angry. You do not have the devil in you, and I'm so sorry that you were treated that way." He hugged me tight, pressing my cheek to his. Pop-pop's arms felt safe and I didn't want to let go.

I sighed. Everything was all so confusing. Why would Ed say that if he didn't see it in me? I know Pop-pop loves me, so he would probably love me even if I did have the devil in me. I couldn't shake the worry that the devil was literally inside me possessing me and stealthily instilling evil into my heart.

"Thanks, Pops. I love you," I said as I licked my finger and ran it across my plate to collect the last of the crumbs. "I just don't want Ed to hurt Mommy or Maddie or me ever, ever again."

He took my hand and made a promise I prayed he'd be able to keep, "I'll never let him hurt you ever again, Doll."

CHAPTER NINE

The next morning, after falling asleep on the couch in the living room watching John Wayne movies with Pop-pop, I woke to the smell of bacon cooking. Wiping the sleep out of my eyes, I headed toward the delicious aroma.

"Good morning, baby," Mom-mom said as she stood over the stove frying bacon.

"Morning, Mom-mom!" I said, sitting down at the kitchen table. "Can I help you with anything?"

"Nope, Maddie already made the toast and your mother handled the coffee pot and now they're upstairs getting dressed. Have some toast."

I helped myself to some toast. Maddie had carefully cut some of the slices into hearts. I took one heart-shaped slice and one regular slice and sat back down.

Staring at the heart-shaped slice of toast, I thought, *I love my sister. Sometimes she gets on my nerves, but if anyone ever tried to hurt her, I would do whatever I could to defend her.* I hoped my mother would do the same for us.

"Mornin' Lissy! Aren't you going to get dressed?" Maddie asked as she danced into the kitchen to a tune in her head. Not waiting for an answer, she grabbed a piece of toast and shoved it in her mouth all at once. Instead of joining me at the table, she hugged Mom-mom and ran out of the kitchen and up the stairs to play in the playroom.

Next to come through the doorway was my mother. When I saw her face, I burst into tears. Her left eye was swollen nearly shut and there were blood vessels broken in her eye. Her cheek was twice its normal size and discolored by fresh bruising.

"Oh, Mommy! Look what he did to your face!" I said, crying. I hugged her tight around her waist and sobbed into her belly.

She choked back tears and said, "It's okay, Lissy. I'm alright and it will heal."

"I hate him! I don't ever want him to hurt you again. Let's never go back there. Please? Can we stay with Mom-mom?" I cried even harder as the scene of Ed punching my mother played like a movie in my mind.

My mother put her hand to my chin and pulled my face up to look at hers. "Lissy, what Ed did was very wrong and I know you don't understand some of the grown-up stuff, but Ed has apologized for everything. He wants us to come home and be a family again. He'll be here soon to talk to you girls and apologize to you directly. I think Ed deserves a second chance, and I'd like to give it to him."

I ripped away from her arms. I couldn't believe what she was saying. I felt so betrayed. Anger rose up through my chest and pulsed through my body into my head, threatening to shoot my head wide open. I had never before experienced such rage.

"Are you serious?" I asked. "Why did he do this? Did you ask him? Is he going to hear my feelings? He RIPPED out my hair and ruined your face!"

I turned my back to her, ran my fingers over my scalp until I felt the sting, and separated my hair, exposing the area where I had discovered a bald spot during a midnight bathroom trip. Turning back toward her, hearing nothing but silence, I searched her face for any hint of compassion for my pain only to find nothing.

"Ed is very sorry, Lissy. I don't know what to tell you. He had a little too much to drink and things got out of hand. I shouldn't have attacked him when he came in the door. None of this would have happened if I had controlled myself. I'm sorry you were hurt, Lissy. Your hair will grow back, and Ed will make it up to you." She said with finality, signaling the end of our conversation and taking a seat at the kitchen table.

I looked at Mom-mom for some sort of support, but when I met her eyes, she turned away.

What the hell is wrong with these people? I don't forgive him. I thought.

I felt helpless and alone. I didn't want to talk to Ed. I was angry. I didn't want to hear anything he had to say. What could he possibly say to make things right? 'Sorry I punched your mother in the face, ripped a bunch of hair out of your head, and said you had the devil in you'? That's not good enough for me. That doesn't ensure my future safety or Maddie's. I didn't really care too much about my mother's safety in my angry state since she was putting us right back into that situation.

Whatever, I thought, *I'll listen to him, but I'm not promising forgiveness.*

I suddenly wasn't feeling very hungry so I decided to skip breakfast and head upstairs to get dressed.

*   *   *   *   *

Maddie was sitting cross-legged on the floor in the playroom with the cat blanket beside her and her favorite teddy bear, Boom-Boom, in her lap. She was coloring in a coloring book and had dressed herself in her frilly pink Easter dress, purple tights, and black rain boots. In her hair, she had carefully tucked a fake yellow flower underneath her bright blue glitter headband.

"Did Mommy talk to you about Ed?" I asked.

"Yes, she did," Maddie replied, "and I think it's alright if he apologizes. He didn't mean it and he said he won't do it again so he better not because that was really scary."

I was starting to feel like I wasn't being reasonable. Everyone else was ready and willing to forgive him for his mistake; why wasn't I?

*   *   *   *   *

When Ed arrived at Mom-mom's house, everyone had a talk downstairs in the living room except for me; I sat in the playroom and waited for him to come to me to say whatever it was he wanted to say. I wasn't going to go out of my way to be apologized to. I sat drawing a picture of a girl's face: no girl in particular, just a girl. I loved to draw eyes and girls had long lashes. As I sat with my back toward the door, concentrating hard on drawing lush feathery lashes, Ed knocked on the open door to get my attention. I didn't turn around.

"Lissy, can I please talk to you?" Ed asked.

"Yes, you may talk to me." I still refused to turn and face him. "I'm listening."

What I really wanted to say was, '*Nobody wants to see your stupid face, Ed. Nobody likes you, especially me. Maybe YOU have the devil in you.*' I decided to keep those words to myself because if I said that, I'd be no better than he would.

"Lissy, I'm very sorry for everything that happened last night. I know you're too young to understand, but sometimes adults drink alcohol and sometimes they drink entirely too much and lose control of their tempers. What you saw last night was my loss of control after drinking too much. I love you, Maddie, and your mother and I'm so sorry and ashamed of my actions. All I want is for you all to forgive me for my huge mistake and for us to be a family again." Ed explained.

He sounded as if he were telling the truth. I truly believed he was honestly sorry for his actions; however, I didn't find any comfort in his apology. His apology was sincere, but could he promise this would never happen again?

"I accept your apology, Ed." I replied. I turned around to look at him and said, "I guess we can all try to be a family again."

Ed smiled a gracious grin. "Thank you, Lissy. I'll prove to you all that I can be the husband your mother needs and the father you and Maddie deserve. I am so very sorry."

He started toward me, possibly for a hug, but I turned my back to him and he stopped. I didn't want him to hug me. I began scribbling over my drawing in dark circles.

"Okay, Lissy. I'll let you be. You have every right to be mad at me. I'll give you some time to cool down. I love you, Lissy. I'll never hurt you ever again."

As he stepped out of the doorway and walked down the hall, I felt extremely confused. I had so many questions. Did this mean that Ed was going to stop drinking? Did he really mean it when he said I had the devil in me? Was my mom mad at me for not being forgiving? Did Mom-mom realize how scared I was to go back there?

I felt like there wasn't anyone who could answer my questions. Mom-mom seemed to be stepping back to allow my mother to handle the situation her way and Pop-pop was doing the best he could to explain things to me, and my mother didn't seem to be able to answer my questions without getting mad at me. Her only answer was to just forgive Ed and give him another chance.

Fine. I thought. *I'll give him his chance but I don't believe for one second that he won't get drunk and do this again.*

CHAPTER TEN

The weeks following Ed's drunken tirade were surprisingly (to me) very happy ones. Ed and my mother were in love all over again; it was as if they had just met and were in the "honeymoon" phase of relationships. Ed was the absolute perfect father to Maddie and me and put out a lot of extra effort to regain our trust and faith in him.

We were a family again and as fall turned into winter, we planned plenty of exciting family events for Christmas. Our mother had to work on Christmas Day, but we had her the entire day on Christmas Eve. This meant she was able to join us at Mom-mom and Pop-pop's annual Christmas Eve party.

On Christmas Eve, Maddie and I got dressed in our matching red and green plaid Christmas dresses Mom-mom had bought us. She loved to dress us up like dolls and styled us up as Shirley Temple clones with curls in our hair, white ruffled socks, and white patent leather dress shoes. Mom-mom had also bought the same exact outfit for our cousin Annabelle, who was just three months older than

Maddie and I. The three of us were regularly mistaken for triplets whenever Mom-mom and Pop-pop took us out together.

Annabelle was our favorite cousin and my best friend, aside from Maddie, of course. She was a beautiful little girl whose Irish features made her look like a porcelain doll. She had long dark brown hair down to her waist, fair skin peppered with freckles and striking light blue eyes. Maddie, Annabelle, and I were practically inseparable before my mother married Ed.

My Uncle Nick and Aunt Roxie, Annabelle's parents, used to take us down the shore every summer and nearly every weekend year-round to Atlantic City where Mom-mom and Pop-pop, Uncle Nick and Aunt Roxie, and the three of us girls would stay at one of the casinos. Annabelle, Maddie, and I would play in the arcades, watch movies, play with our Barbie dolls, or swim in the pool while the adults gambled. At least one of them was with us at all times. They took turns staying with us while the others gambled, but Aunt Roxie seemed to be with us the most.

Uncle Nick was my mom's younger brother and he was a fun guy. Aunt Roxie, his wife, was the love of his life and they had a great relationship. Uncle Nick was the best father and the definition of a good man. He loved his wife and his children and would do anything for them. Though he could appear a tough guy, he had a huge heart and was fiercely protective of his family.

Many times in my life, I wished Uncle Nick and Aunt Roxie were my parents. I loved my mother to death, but sometimes I wished to be part of a happy family who spent time together and went on vacation together and genuinely enjoyed spending time together.

Still, I was thankful for my mother. She did her best to give us the best life she could possibly give us and for that I ~~should be~~ am grateful.

"Do you girls have your shoes on?" My mother asked. "Are you guys ready to go?" She was excited for the party. I loved seeing her smile.

"Yes, Mommy, we're all set! I can't wait to see Annabelle! Do you think Aunt Roxie made cookies this year? I hope Pop-pop wears his Santa hat!" I said, as I put my arms into my white faux-fur dress coat, also courtesy of Mom-mom.

"So many questions! You're excited, huh?" She giggled at me as she helped Maddie into her coat, which was identical to mine, of course.

"Yes!" I exclaimed. "But where's Ed, Mommy? Is he coming?"

"Ed's going to meet us there in a little while; he had to work late, but will be there before we open presents."

We always exchanged gifts with our Aunts, Uncles, and cousins on Christmas Eve at around nine o'clock after eating appetizers and watching Christmas movies.

"Okay, then. Let's go!" I marched toward the door like a soldier. Maddie, who was in the middle of being primped by my mother, wrestled free from her grasp and followed me in-step.

"Let's go!" Maddie mimicked.

My mother grabbed her purse and the gifts for my cousins, and out the door we marched.

*   *   *   *   *

When we arrived at Mom-mom's, we stared in awe at the Christmas lights outside. Pop-pop had done a spectacular job with the lights that year.

"Wow!" Maddie said. "There's no way Santa would miss this house with these lights."

"No way!" I said in agreement.

We gathered the gifts for my cousins and went up to the door, all three of us knocking cheerfully at the same time, attempting the rhythm of Jingle Bells but not quite succeeding.

"Hi, Dolls. Merry Christmas!" said Mom-mom as she opened the door.

"Merry Christmas!" We all said in unison.

Annabelle came running to the door when she heard our voices.

"Hi, Aunt Anna! Maddie, Lissy; come on! You have to see the tree. Pop-pop let me put the angel on top!" Annabelle didn't wait for us; she was too excited. She ran to the living room and Maddie and I hurried to catch up to her.

The tree was beautiful; it was lovingly decorated with the same ornaments Mom-mom used every year. Of course, it wasn't a real tree; oh no, those were too messy. Mom-mom put up the same plastic tree every year on Black Friday and all of the family members would hang an ornament or two when they visited from that time until Christmas Eve;

then, on Christmas Eve, one of the younger children would get to put the angel on top. Maddie and I did it the year before, so Annabelle did it that year.

"Great job, Annabelle!" I praised. "It's not even crooked or anything."

Beaming proudly, she said, "Thanks, Lissy. Pop-pop had to lift me up there, and I was shaking a little bit, but I think I did a good job."

We both stared at the tree, mesmerized by the bright white twinkle lights that lit up the vintage red and gold ball ornaments that were scattered throughout the tree in between the keepsake ornaments.

"Guys, let's watch *Santa Claus Is Coming to Town*. Pop-pop put it on the TV for us." Maddie said, breaking the trance the tree had on me.

"Okay! That's my favorite Christmas Special." I said.

"Mine too!" said Annabelle.

The three of us grabbed some cookies Aunt Roxie had made for the party and sat down in front of the TV as close as we could get away with without being yelled at. As we watched our specials, the rest of our family enjoyed the get-together.

Looking around the room, I saw Aunt Roxie and my mother laughing heartily, Pop-pop and Uncle Nick sipping beer and looking serious, and Mom-mom and my mother's sister, Aunt Sandy talking very dramatically about something that looked like sad news. Two of my older cousins, Kristin and Jasmine, were standing near the food chatting away while my teenage cousins, Alex and Brandon, were trying to sneak beer from the fridge.

It was a great Christmas Eve and I felt so cozy and happy visiting with my family members, eating Christmas cookies, watching the Christmas TV Specials, and listening to Christmas music while feeling the excitement of waiting for Santa Claus to come.

*   *   *   *   *

A loud series of urgent knocks on the front door pulled my attention immediately away from the TV. Maddie, Annabelle, and I looked at each other in excitement wondering in unison if Santa had come early. Doubtful, I dismissed that thought since of course we had to be asleep for him to come, so obviously it wasn't Santa Claus. I shook my head at Maddie and Annabelle, who got the message. Since it wasn't Santa, they turned their attention back to the program; the only thing more exciting than Christmas specials was Santa himself.

Uncle Nick raised his hand signaling to everyone that he'd answer the door. Curious as to who was there, I followed him out to the foyer to see. I tiptoed as quietly as I could out of the living room, through the kitchen, and onto the marble floor of the foyer in my dress shoes, attempting to maintain a safe distance behind Uncle Nick. I felt like a private detective sneaking behind him on my mission to identify the person who had knocked on the door, stealthily watching, and investigating.

When he opened the door, Uncle Nick stepped back suddenly when the visitor at the door stumbled in with hands full of wreaths.

"Whoa, look who finally made it!" said Uncle Nick in a friendly tone. It was Ed. My excitement waned as soon as I

53

heard him speak.

"Yep! I'm here now- and the kiddos wanna have sum wreaths for Christmas so I brang a bunch for 'em," he said, slurring his words in drunk-man speak complete with odd sounding S's. He struggled with the numerous wreaths in his arms and dropped fresh pine needles everywhere.

"Let me help you with those before Bette has a fit about the mess they make." Uncle Nick knew Mom-mom would not have a Merry Christmas if her house weren't spotless. "Let's take these out to the garage and bring everyone out to see them," he instructed.

Uncle Nick headed out the front door to lead Ed to the outdoor entrance of the garage on the side of the house while I retreated to the living room where the family Christmas party was still on.

In the living room, the door that led to the garage swung open and Uncle Nick popped his head through.

"C'mon, everybody! Ed is here and he's brought us all something special," he announced.

Everyone followed him into the garage where he had laid out the wreaths on a blue tarp so that no mess was made of Mom-Mom's freshly vacuumed carpeted garage floor.

"Wow, Ed, thank you for this nice gift!" All things Ed brought from his farm always impressed Aunt Roxie.

I have to admit; I do think it's cool that he grows so many things himself that most people buy from supermarkets. I suppose I take for granted the fact that I can go in my backyard and pick a peach to eat in the summer, or pick a pumpkin from my own land in the fall, or watch my Christmas tree grow; seeing my family's delight over the homegrown and handmade goods reminded me to be grateful for that.

"I want this one," said Annabelle, pointing to the largest, most lush wreath.

"Then it shall be for you, kiddo," Ed said.

I became annoyed when he referred to Annabelle as "kiddo." His inebriated niceties weren't winning me over, but they seemed to be affecting the rest of my family members in the intended way; everyone was gushing over his wreaths like groupies. I felt hurt that they all thought he was so nice when they didn't know who he really was; or, rather, who he became when he got drunk past the point of "kiddo."

I searched the room for my mother, wondering what her reaction was to Ed's display of, in my opinion, sickeningly sweet generosity. When I found her, she was staring at Ed with white-hot rage, and I finally understood the meaning of the phrase, 'If looks could kill...'

While they all took turns choosing a wreath and discussed ideas for decorating them, I retreated back to the living room to savor just a bit more of the Christmas cheer before I had to go home to the chaotic holiday I knew I was inevitably going to have at home.

CHAPTER ELEVEN

"You're drunk, aren't you?" My mother asked Ed as we arrived home, before we even finished getting through the door; I had no clue why she was asking when it was more than obvious that he was, and he wasn't going to admit it.

"No, I am not drunk, Anna. I had two beers. You are crazy!"

The very last shred of hope I'd been hanging onto that a fight could have been avoided evaporated immediately. They launched into a full-scale verbal assault, and though I tried to muster up the will to back up my mother, I just couldn't do it. I walked away and tried my best to block out all of the commotion.

As they continued attacking each other with colorful profanities, I dropped the gifts I had received from my aunts and uncles under tree and Maddie did the same. We took off our dress coats and hung them up in the closet by the front door as Ed and my mother moved their altercation into the kitchen.

Though I felt like I should do something to help my

mother, I didn't feel like getting involved in their battle. It was Christmas, after all, and it was supposed to be a special, happy day. Did they have to do this now? Why did my mother have to ask him if he was drunk? She knew he was drunk, what good could it have possibly done to confront him about it?

Maddie had settled down in front of the tree and pulled out one of her new Barbie dolls. She too was ignoring the fight and instead was lovingly brushing her doll's hair. I was surprised the doll still had its original outfit on, as Maddie always changed her dolls' clothes immediately after tearing open the package. She was very interested in fashion design and had her own unique style that she could never wait to impose upon her dolls, yet she had kept this doll dressed as it had come packaged.

"How come you didn't change that doll's clothes, Maddie? I asked. "You always have them in new outfits right away."

"I just want to keep this doll the way she is. She looks happy like that, so I'd rather not change her," she responded in a somber tone.

It made sense to me that she'd keep that particular doll 'the way she was' in her original outfit. The doll was uniformed in a white nurse's dress that looked exactly like the one our mother had worn at her graduation from Nursing School, complete with white nurse's cap, white stockings, white shoes, and black stethoscope. The doll reminded Maddie of our mother, and the permanent smile she wore would remind Maddie that there were happier times for our mother, ones that made her smile instead of cry, and laugh instead of scream.

"Alright then, keep her that way. At least she isn't *naked*!" I teased; giggling knowing that nude was a common state for her dolls to be in when she got frustrated with planning an outfit or their hair behaving. "Let's go get in our pajamas and get ready for Santa Claus!"

"OK!" She said, as she grabbed her doll and a candy cane from her pile of gifts. "Let's go before he gets here and we're not asleep. He'll pass right by!"

"I know, let's go!" I said, shoving one of Aunt Roxie's homemade cookies I had stowed away in my pocket into my mouth and running toward the stairs to beat Maddie to our room.

I nearly choked on cookie crumbs racing Maddie up the stairs with my mouth full, laughing with excitement. Our cheeks flushed red, we both got to the bedroom at almost the same time, with Maddie ahead of me only slightly, though I would have beaten her if she didn't push me when we rounded the corner arriving on the second floor. Maddie fought dirty, but I didn't mind. For me, competition was fun and the outcome of winning or losing didn't matter, especially since I won the majority of competitions against Maddie.

Twins are extremely competitive since there's always someone there to challenge you every minute of your life; you must share everything, and some people treat you as one person, which is a bit offensive when you both know you're two completely different people and not only one-half of one whole pair of twins.

"I won!" exclaimed Maddie victoriously. She beamed with pride.

"Yeah, yeah, you win, I lose, now let's go to sleep before

Santa passes our house!"

We put on our new Christmas nightgowns, pulled out the trundle bed from underneath our shared daybed, and hopped in for sleep.

As I shut my eyes and prepared to doze off, I heard my mother and Ed still going at it downstairs. Though I wondered if I should go check on my mother, sleep caught me before I could act.

*   *   *   *   *

I awoke in a panic at three o'clock in the morning. I'm not sure exactly what woke me, but as I tiptoed out of my room to the bathroom, I heard a loud bang coming from downstairs.

Is that Santa? I wondered to myself.

I decided to skip my bathroom trip and have a peek to see if I could catch a glimpse of Santa Claus in the flesh. Creeping down the stairs as quietly as I could and holding my breath in excited anticipation of catching Santa in the act of placing our presents under the tree, I stopped mid-step when I heard the faint sound of someone talking, or was that crying? Laughing? I wasn't sure.

As I came closer to the sound, I realized it was a female crying. I feared for a moment that it might be Ed's Aunt Grace in full ghostly regalia coming to chase us out of her house. Terrified at the thought, I felt a strong urge to run frantically up the stairs to my room to hide under the covers. My legs wouldn't move though, so I just stood there, heart in my throat, eyes widened, paralyzed with fear.

"Lissy?"

When the voice said my name, my heart nearly stopped cold in absolute horror until I recognized the voice as my mother's. I sighed in relief and relaxed. I wasn't sure when I had become such a 'scaredy-cat,' but I was a little ashamed of myself for letting my imagination run so wild.

"Mommy? Are you alright?" I asked.

It was dark and I couldn't see her. She was sitting in the living room in the dark with the tree off. Though the Christmas lights on the banister of the stairs had lit my way down, they cast practically no light into the room. My bare foot felt for the cold hardwood floor and I waited for my eyes to adjust to the darkness before I saw her in silhouette form sitting in a chair by the front window.

"I'm ok, Lissy, come over here and give Mommy a hug."

I found my way to her without stubbing any toes and snuggled onto her lap, giving her a great big hug. It had felt like ages since she had given me that much affection. I hadn't realized I missed it so much. I laid my head on her chest and sat there with her for a moment in silence just enjoying being with her.

Remembering I had heard my mother crying, I looked up at her to ask her why she'd been doing so, but stopped when the white Christmas lights sparkling outside shone on her face and revealed swelling on her lip and forehead. Though it didn't look as bad as it had the last time in the dim light, it still hurt me just the same to see my mother that way.

"Mommy!" I sat up in alarm, "Ed hurt you again? Where is he? Did he leave? Did he leave forever?" As I blurted out my tear-filled questions, she nodded, shrugged, nodded, and unfortunately, shook her head 'no' to my last question.

"So he's coming back after he hurt you again? Why?" I didn't know whether to be mad or cry. Since being mad was easier, I chose anger.

"Lissy, you don't understand. I can't raise two little girls on my own. You and Maddie need a father in your lives. Your father didn't want to be a father, but Ed *wants* to be your father. He loves all of us; he just has a drinking problem. He's going to get help. Things will be better, I promise.

I was in total disbelief of every word that was exiting her treasonous mouth. Who was this woman and what did she do with my real mother? My cheeks were hot with fury and I could feel myself balling my fists in rage, nails digging firmly into my palms.

"I do NOT need a father and neither does Maddie; we have Mom-mom and Pop-pop and Uncle Nick and Aunt Roxie. We have lots of people in our lives who love us and don't hurt us! We do not need Ed, Mommy. We can go live with Mom-mom and Pop-pop and be happy again. It will be me, you, and Maddie just the three of us again and we can be happy!"

I was desperate for her to agree with me and terribly furious with her for thinking any of us would be safe or happy living with Ed any longer.

"No, Lissy. We are not going to live with Mom-mom and Pop-pop again," she stated angrily and firmly, nudging me to get up off her lap. "Ed and I are married and when you marry someone, you stay by their side through better or worse. You cannot just leave when things get rough, you have to work through things and make them better together."

In total disbelief, I just stood there staring at my mother. Marriage sounded like an awful deal if you had to stay with someone who was beating you up just because you promised to be there through everything- good and bad. If all of this was true, I was never getting married. It had to be true, though, right? Otherwise, why would someone put up with such treatment?

I realized my mother had her mind made up; Ed and his drinking problem were here to stay, for better or worse. I sincerely hoped it didn't get much worse.

CHAPTER TWELVE

That Christmas morning was tense for me, but Ed had come home sometime after I went back to bed and made up with my mother. They were smiling and joking all morning as if nothing had happened the night before. I didn't know how my mother could forgive him so easily, or how he could look at her, bruised and swollen, and not hate himself for what he'd done to her. Maybe he did hate himself, but I didn't think so. I think he believed "I'm sorry" fixed everything.

I went through the motions of opening presents and taking pictures, but truly, I was only feigning excitement. I had noticed during my middle of the night chat with my mother that Santa had already come, but I didn't care; I was too upset with my mother and Ed. After talking with my mother, I had gotten no sleep; there was entirely too much on my mind.

Lying in my bed that night after my chat with my mother, I found myself staring at the ceiling, pondering several truly disturbing scenarios that could possibly arise because of my mother's choice to stay with Ed despite his angry drunken tirades. Considering his recent violent outburst directed at my mother's face, what I feared most was that he would kill her; or me, or Maddie.

In spite of my unfamiliarity with the cycle of abuse at the time, I had a feeling that what was happening would only get worse and that the changes I'd recently seen in my once happy, smiling, confident, strong mother would only become more drastic. I feared for her wellness, as well as Maddie's and my own. I only hoped my mother cared for ours in the same way.

*   *   *   *   *

Days and months passed with no change in the routine of chaos in our home; Ed would get drunk, fight with my mother, we'd escape to Mom-mom's for the night, and the next day they'd pretend nothing happened and we'd all just play along.

I came to find ways to protect Maddie and myself during the times where they fought and tried to drag us into it. I'd sometimes succeed in drowning out their shouts and screams with music, while other times I'd fail miserably and go crazy on Ed while he beat up my mother, which usually left me with less hair on my head and some bruises. In general, Ed didn't really put his hands on us in a violent manner, but if I got in between the physical fights he had with my mother, he would hit me or pull my hair and say awful things to me.

Unfortunately, I had been right in my prediction that things with Ed would only get worse. Because of my mother's decision to stay with Ed despite the turmoil he created, Maddie and I felt extremely betrayed by her. We didn't feel that we could talk to her about anything, and if we told her we were sad, or mad, or hurt, she dismissed our feelings and became resentful of our needs. Her favorite speech to give us when we were sad was, "Get over it. There are people in the world who have things way worse than you, so be grateful that you have a roof over your head, clothes on your back, and food in your stomach."

We were grateful for those things, I assured her repeatedly, but what she didn't seem to understand is that we would have traded anything in the world to have our mother back the way she was before she married Ed. She had changed drastically and we missed the ways she used to be; she had stopped being a mother to us and spent most of her time consumed with what Ed was doing.

Aside from neglecting us, she was also neglecting herself. She no longer seemed to put as much effort into her hobbies, she gained weight, and she smoked and ate as if it were her last day on Earth. She withdrew from her family and friends and worked double shifts at work as often as she could; partially to escape from the misery at home, but also to make up for Ed's financial irresponsibility; he'd get drunk and spend the money for the electric bill, phone bill, or mortgage payment and leave my mother to clean up the mess. Even though Ed went to work every day and earned a decent living, he preferred to spend his earnings on beer.

Ed was also changing, and not for the better in any sense of the matter. He was increasingly becoming more violent as time passed, and as Maddie and I got older, directed it at us.

I was roughly eight years old when Ed first became

physically violent with me outside of a fight with my mother. That day began like most others with my mother at work when Maddie and I got off school and our usual routine with Mom-mom afterward. When Ed picked us up that evening, he was drunk as he was most evenings, and the ride home with him was terrifying as always, Ed swerving on the road and me praying to God that we'd make it home alive.

When we got home that night, Ed did what he usually did, took a shower, and ate whatever meal my mother had prepared and left for him in the fridge while Maddie and I finished our homework and completed our chores. After our work was complete, we showered and dressed for bed, then headed out to the kitchen for a snack.

Maddie and I always had a snack before bed, usually cereal, fruit, or yogurt. Though we were not allowed to have soda or any sugary drinks, we were permitted to drink water or juice with our snack. This particular night, we had cereal and Ed informed us that we could only drink water with our cereal because it was sugary and we had milk in our cereal to drink.

I had every intention of following his orders, however, when I opened the fridge to get the milk for our cereal, I saw a bottle of cream soda my mother had bought for herself and decided that, because it was clear like water, I'd play a prank on Ed. My plan was to pour cream soda in my glass instead of water and have Ed investigate as to why my water was so sweet. I thought it would be funny to see him respond to the unexpected sweet taste.

I poured myself a glass and sat down at the kitchen table next to Maddie, who was almost done her bowl of cereal, and began eating my cereal as I waited for Ed to come check on us as he usually did to make sure we didn't make a mess.

When Ed entered the kitchen, I had a mouthful of cereal and wasn't prepared to play my prank on him. Before I could swallow my food, he noticed the carbonation in my "water."

"What is this?" Ed asked sternly, pointing to my glass.

"It's water." I said with a nervous giggle. Something told me this prank was about to backfire on me in a very bad way.

He took a sip of the drink, swished it around in his mouth for a moment, looking from me, to the glass, back to me. I became very uneasy due to his serious demeanor and lost the courage to carry out my prank, though that may not have been the best idea because Ed took great offense to my acting against his authority and insulting his intelligence.

"This is cream soda." He stated in an accusatory tone that made me realize that backing out of my prank made me look like a sneaky liar who was trying to get one over on him.

My face flushed bright red in embarrassment, and for some reason, perhaps out of fear of his reaction if I admitted the truth, I said, "No it's not."

I have no clue why I thought that would be a good answer, or why I didn't see how denying the truth was going to make anything better, but I had said it and there was no taking it back.

Ed threw the soda all over me, covering my clean pajamas and freshly washed hair, as well as the table and floor. Maddie froze in her seat, shocked at his actions. I was humiliated tremendously and felt stupid for having thought the prank would be funny, but also by having been too intimidated by Ed to carry it out. I sat there with one eye open, soda dripping into the other, waiting for Ed to strike me. I knew he was going to; I felt it in my gut and braced myself for the impact.

Sure enough, seconds later, I felt my head snap back as he pulled me by my hair out of my chair; with one hand holding my hair, he was removing his belt with the other. Once removed, he looped it up in half and began hitting me hard anywhere he could gain access.

The leather belt stung harshly as it made contact with my bare arms and legs, leaving ugly red welts behind. I curled up in a ball on the floor and covered my face as best as I could while he still had a firm grip on my hair. I took each hit with acceptance and shame, feeling awful for my mistake and hating myself for being so stupid as to think my joke would be funny. I felt I deserved what I was getting because I had done something wrong.

I heard Maddie yelling, "Stop, Ed! Please stop!"

"Go in the bedroom, Maddie, just go!" I shouted to her.

Tears dripping down her frantic face, Maddie hesitated, wondering if she should risk her own safety by defending me, then followed my instructions to leave, and ran out of the room. Maddie having to see me get beaten made me feel worse about my stupid prank; I knew how hard it was to watch someone you love be hurt and feel helpless.

"You fucking little cunt bitch! You're a liar and a sneak. Do you think I'm fucking stupid?" He screamed loudly, hitting me harder with each syllable.

Beating me with the belt appeared to give Ed some sort of sadistic satisfaction. His face bore a look of someone who was not only thrilled by the act he was performing, but also disturbingly gratified; almost like a drug addict getting their fix after a period of painful withdrawal symptoms. I wasn't sure how much longer I'd have to endure his wrath before he got his "fix."

Finally, he relented. "Spic bitch," he said, spitting in my face and releasing my hair from his grasp with one final push of my head into the floor. He rolled up his belt and walked away, looking proud of himself and liberated from the insult to his intelligence.

At the time, I didn't know what a spic was, but it sounded to me like a bad thing to be, and it made me feel worthless. I later found out what it meant to be a spic during an intense argument with my cousin Annabelle over whose Barbie doll was allowed to drive the Barbie car we shared, so I called her a spic in front of Mom-mom. As one could imagine, this didn't go over well and not only did I receive a punishment, I also received a lesson in racial slurs: Spics were Hispanic people, and yes, I was technically one of them.

CHAPTER THIRTEEN

I told Mom-mom and Pop-pop about the cream soda incident with Ed. Though they listened to me and attempted to give me support, they didn't seem sure I was completely telling the truth. They brought my story to my mother's attention, but she vehemently denied Ed would ever lay a hand on us kids unless it was for punishment. After speaking to my mother, Mom-mom and Pop-pop sat me down and explained to me that Ed had hit me with a belt because I had lied and that he was only disciplining me for my wrongdoing.

My grandparents' response crushed me inside; I had thought that perhaps they'd understand how badly it made me feel and how excessive I felt his punishment was. Still, I trusted their judgment because I believed they knew what was best for me. Perhaps I had deserved it. Although I hadn't ever had to be disciplined like that before Ed came around, I accepted their word as truth and relied upon that moving forward. I told myself that Ed was only trying to teach me right from wrong, and I just needed to be good and do the right things so that Ed wouldn't have to hit me like that again.

From that day on, I made every attempt to be a good little girl; I did my chores as asked, my homework without complaining, and did my best to make sure Maddie also complied without fuss as well. I got excellent grades in school and though Maddie usually was an average student, she began improving her grades as well.

Maddie and I tried very hard to be perfect, well-behaved little girls, but Ed still "disciplined" us regularly for various, often unknown reasons. Sometimes our hair was wrong, sometimes we chewed too loud, and other times it wasn't clear what we had done wrong; all we knew was that it was something we did that caused Ed to lash out at us the way he did.

My mother explained away Ed's form of discipline as a father's way of handling children. I decided early on that fathers were awful and I'd never make my children have one. No matter how much time passed, I couldn't be convinced that having a father was a good thing because it made our lives so hellish. Our mother showed no compassion for our feelings on the matter or concern for our safety, so I didn't feel supported or like anyone believed me. I felt extremely alone and unloved as a result and felt I had no adult in my corner to defend Maddie and me. I just wanted someone to agree that this was wrong. Maybe I was blowing things out of proportion, but I didn't feel I was; the situation felt wrong on many levels.

Living with the constant worry of being disciplined for sometimes-unclear reasons, I became an anxious and insecure child and began picking at my appearance and focusing on everything bad inside me. My self-esteem suffered and I felt like the ugly, stupid, idiotic, loser fat girl Ed accused me of being on a regular basis. When someone tells you every day how awful you are, you come to believe it, no matter how strong or confident you are, especially if that someone is a person who's supposed to love you and treat you well.

Hopelessness and helplessness turned me inward and I withdrew from my family and friends. I felt unworthy of friendship and love, a feeling I still struggle with on a daily basis to this very day. It's hard to reverse feelings of worthlessness after the damage of emotional abuse. I'd much rather be beaten to a bloody pulp than to be told what an ugly, fat, disgusting loser I am. Bruises and cuts may take some time to heal, but emotional scars linger the longest.

Books saved me during the hardest times of my childhood. They provided other worlds and lives I could escape to where people loved each other, families didn't hurt each other, and girls my age did fun things like have slumber parties and play sports. I'd read the Sweet Valley Twins series and pretend I was part of their family. I pictured the twins as Maddie and me, and pretended the fictional parents were my real parents. Soothing words of compassion and love from the parents in the book were often highlighted so I could read them to myself whenever I was in need of comfort; it helped a lot to make-believe I had someone in this world on my side.

Having books in my life helped, but they were not a permanent solution to my problems. Oftentimes Ed would catch me reading long after he'd made us go to bed and turn the lights out. I'd usually make the mistake of believing he was asleep and sit at my bedroom window trying to read books by the light of the porch lamp outside. Our bedroom door was never allowed to be closed, so Ed would walk past my door and catch me in the act. His response was generally to drag me by my hair back to bed and rip my books to shreds.

Since most of my books came from my school library, my parents always had to pay to replace them when they were destroyed, but that didn't stop Ed from doing it. However, it did cause the school library to stop lending me books, which took a vital survival tool away from me. I'm sure the school librarian didn't know how important books were to me, or why the books I borrowed usually ended up destroyed, but books were something I desperately needed in order to have some sort of joy in my life. Once I lost my literary portal to other worlds, I felt very disconnected from all happiness.

To isolate us even more from the world, my mother had put an end to our weekend trips to Atlantic City with Mom-mom and Pop-pop. She believed that Uncle Nick and Aunt Roxie asked too many questions about our home life, which they did surely out of concern, but in my mother's eyes, this was prying. She believed her family judged her decisions as a mother and Ed helped convinced her of this.

Spending less time with family, losing my escape to fictional destinations, and having to spend all of my free time walking on eggshells around Ed wore me down emotionally. I felt as if I was dying inside and that I didn't have anything to look forward to in life. Depression consumed me, and I allowed it. I was convinced that nothing in the world could ever make me feel good or happy again.

To my pleasant surprise, I learned soon after that I was wrong; I did indeed have something wonderful to look forward to and be happy about. I was going to be a big sister! My mother and Ed were going to have a baby boy, and he was due to arrive in a few short months. They had already decided on a name: David James Adams. I could hardly wait to meet him.

CHAPTER FOURTEEN

Just before my tenth birthday, my little brother David was born. He came into this world a healthy, happy baby and I fell in love with him instantly. Though I thought he looked like an alien his first week home and was terrified of breaking him, I wanted to hold him in my arms forever. Seeing his tiny fingers wrapped around one of my own big-kid sized fingers gave me a feeling of joy and love I never knew I could experience.

From the beginning, David became my real-life baby doll. I enjoyed feeding him, singing to him, playing with him, changing him, and all of the things required when caring for an infant. I was never one who was interested in baby dolls or babies; in fact, babies scared me and I hated when they screamed or cried and I always preferred Barbie dolls over baby dolls because Barbie dolls were fabulous and baby dolls were boring. I felt differently about David. I felt a connection with him and didn't see him as a little crying bundle of poop as I did with most other babies. David had a vibrant personality from the start; he was full of smiles and curiosity, as well as an obvious eagerness to learn everything.

David's entrance into my world brought me back to life inside. I began feeling positive emotions again and couldn't wait to get home every day from school to see him. I loved to make him smile, blow spit bubbles, or watch him sleep peacefully, and caring for him gave me a reason to look forward to each new day.

As David grew older, Maddie and I both enjoyed teaching him things; there was a unique satisfaction to being the first person in a child's life to show them something new, or to see them do something own their own for the first time. For me, it was very rewarding to teach David to say he was sorry when he made a mistake or hurt my feelings. In our house, "I'm sorry," was a phrase rarely used even when it was warranted, and I wanted David to learn that he should say he was sorry when he did something wrong, and that he could say so and have his feelings respected- by me, at least.

I loved being a big sister to David, and both of my siblings were extremely important to me. This fact became a big problem, however, when my parents would engage in their usual bloodbaths. I not only had Maddie to protect, but David as well, which became a rather large burden for my young soul to bear.

The majority of the first few years of David's life were very dysfunctional. It was obvious to everyone in my family, including me, that Ed hadn't truly wanted to be a father. He believed my mother had gotten pregnant on purpose to trap him, an accusation that made roughly no sense at all considering they were married and had been together for six years prior to David's birth. Nonetheless, Ed openly resented my mother and his drinking binges became heavier and more frequent.

My mother also increasingly became more hostile toward us, yet more devoted to Ed. The worse he treated her, the more she desired his acceptance and love, and the worse she treated us. Our home life was constantly tumultuous and my mother went back and forth between playing the role as Ed's best friend and ally against us children when she and Ed were in love, to being our best friend and wonderful mother when she and Ed were fighting. It was extremely confusing and very painful when she suddenly switched from our greatest friend to our worst enemy. She would do anything and act any way to please Ed.

Though we were invited to go to Mom-mom's house as usual after school, Maddie and I began going to our own house after school to be with David while my mother and Ed worked. Ed would work on the farm until about nine o'clock at night and my mother wouldn't get home until eleven. This meant that we were responsible for our own dinner and for keeping the house clean, but these responsibilities usually fell on me, being the most capable child.

Either Maddie was the laziest, most helpless child in the world, or she was a genius who knew how to feign uselessness to get out of doing chores. I'm sure it was the latter, as over the years, she has proved herself more than capable when she wants something. Regardless, I was the one most eager to help my mother and to step up as the mother hen, so I did the housework and made sure we all had dinner, did our homework, and got to bed before Ed came home.

Most nights we did a decent job of caring for ourselves; except for the time I broke my foot doing a cartwheel in my bedroom (I have no idea where that dresser came from) and the time I set the stove on fire frying chicken. In my defense, a toddling David had run through the kitchen stark naked after pooping on the potty and I got distracted, but we made out well overall, in my opinion, for three kids practically raising themselves.

There were times, though, that I missed doing things other kids did like watch TV or have someone care for them, or play outside, or have sleepovers. I wasn't able to attend sleepovers because my mother needed me home with David in the evenings. My friends couldn't sleep over my house because my mother couldn't trust how Ed would act in the presence of children and he had a habit of going to bed naked and leaving his bedroom door wide open. When you're a pre-teen girl, that's the last thing you want to see when you wake up in the middle of the night to go to the bathroom.

Though I sometimes resented the role I took on at home as a mother figure to Maddie and David, I felt a responsibility to them to care for them and protect them. I felt they needed me and I feared what would happen to them if I weren't there. Because I knew what went on when I was there, I couldn't imagine how much worse it would be for them if I weren't.

*   *   *   *   *

"Ed, wake up! Mommy's going to be home any minute!" I pushed his shoulder hard to nudge him awake. He had fallen asleep face down in his dinner plate.

No response.

I hope he drowns in his Manicotti.

"Ed, get up NOW!" I yelled.

He sat up straight in his chair with a jolt, putting on a very serious alert face as if he were awake the whole time.

"What? Yes, I know it's Tuesday and you had better have your homework done." He said matter-of-factly and resumed eating his meal as if he wasn't just using it as a pillow.

I noticed ricotta cheese and sauce stuck to his face where it had been laying in his dish and felt satisfied. Ed had come home that evening and decided to make himself some homemade Manicotti using every dish in the house after I had already done the dishes (by hand, I might add- we didn't own a dishwasher). He did so despite the fact that my mother had cooked before she went to work that day and there were plenty of leftovers for him.

I looked around the kitchen at the mess he'd made and sighed. There was no time to clean it all up before my mother got home. She was surely going to have a fit and there was no doubt I'd get the brunt. Ed finished his dinner, wiped his face with his shirt, and stumbled out of the kitchen up to bed leaving his mess behind for me to tend to.

As I gathered up his dishes and placed them in the sink to soak, I couldn't stop myself from breaking down in tears. I was tired- physically and emotionally tired. Tired of cleaning up after a grown man's messes and tired of my mother allowing it. I felt guilty feeling that way because my mother needed my help and my sister and brother needed me too. It felt like a selfish thing to resent them for needing

79

me. Still, it was hard to be happy when everyone needed so much.

When I heard the front door open, I straightened myself up and wiped the tears from my face. I had attempted to straighten up the kitchen as best as possible and to be in the act of washing dishes when my mother walked into the kitchen so she'd not get upset at the mess; I didn't want her to think I hadn't cleaned as I was supposed to.

"What the fuck is this shit?" she asked. "Your lazy ass waiting 'til I came home to do this shit? No, NO! Ed, get your ass down here and tell this girl to do what I asked."

"Mom, I did clean up, but Ed came home and made a mess after I finished," I explained.

"Oh, so it's Ed's fault that you didn't do your chores?" she looked at me, daring me to blame Ed.

"Well..." I wanted to say yes, because technically, it was his fault, but I figured I'd better not. "No."

"Then clean this shit up NOW!" she screamed.

She began throwing everything from the kitchen table onto the floor, making a bigger mess than there had been initially.

I wanted to cry, but I knew it was pointless to do so. Instead, I began cleaning up the mess while my mother kept berating me. At least Maddie and David were in bed and their homework was complete- one less thing to get in trouble for.

When my mother had verbally bashed me to a figurative pulp, she was satisfied and settled down at her normal place at the kitchen table, lit a cigarette, and said, "Make me a cup of coffee."

That was definitely not a request.

.

CHAPTER FIFTEEN

Life continued throughout middle school to be a daily struggle with chores, taking care of my baby brother, cleaning up after a drunken man and trying to avoid being "disciplined," being there for Maddie, and enduring my mother's wrath every night when she got home. School became the lowest priority in my life, as with all my duties at home, there was no time for homework. I loved school and had always been an honor student, but any work that needed doing outside of school hours was impossible for me to complete; thus, by the time I was in eighth grade, my excellent grades fell to terrible grades for the first time in my life.

I tried so many ways to organize myself with school and life, but no matter what, I could not concentrate or organize myself well enough to succeed in both. Who could complete any homework with a child crawling all over their books, Ed ripping up their notebooks, or their mother waking them up at eleven o'clock at night to re-clean things they hadn't cleaned quite the way she wanted? I couldn't.

I'm sure there were kids in my classes who performed poorly in school simply because they didn't really care about school or perhaps had zero interest in learning; I wasn't one of them. Not being able to keep up in school was a huge blow to my self-esteem, as I loved learning, and excelling in school had been one of the last remaining things I had that proved to me that I wasn't a complete piece of crap human being. I was a smart young girl. I wasn't athletic, exceptionally pretty, or amazingly talented; I was a smart kid and losing that part of my identity only solidified my belief that I was indeed a loser, as my parents repeatedly told me.

After failing to maintain a grasp on arguably the most important piece of my sense of self, I began to wonder who I was as a person and started trying on different personalities to see what fit. I went through various phases of social groups: the alternative girl phase; the ghetto girl phase; the Goth girl phase; the preppie phase; and lastly, the slut phase, which unfortunately lasted longer than I like to admit.

I wasn't aware of this fact before middle school, but it's extremely easy to be labeled a slut. All you need is a pair of big boobs, a big butt, or a beautiful face, along with lots of attention from the most coveted boys in school, and voila, you're a slut; this unfortunately happened to me when I hit puberty. The summer before eighth grade, out of the practically indented chest I had the year before, sprung womanly D-cup breasts that my mental maturity wasn't exactly in accord with.

Having the mind of a child and the body of a woman was dangerous in many ways. First, I had no idea my changing body would change the way people treated me. I wasn't prepared for the sudden rise in social status my full chest was garnering me. It was quite shocking to me that I, an invisible nerd only one school year before, was suddenly getting attention from people who never knew I existed based solely on my appearance. I may have looked like a different person on the outside, but I knew I was no different on the inside. I learned a valuable lesson through that change in my appearance; the world treats you better when you're beautiful.

My new womanly figure also caused trouble for me in that suddenly older boys paid attention to me. My naiveté put me in an odd predicament on my first real date at the age of thirteen. The boy I went out with was sixteen and we planned to see a movie and get ice cream afterward. During the movie, we held hands and I thought he was the cutest guy I had ever met in my entire life. I was wondering if he was going to kiss me and felt so nervous and excited in anticipation of my very first kiss!

My excitement vanished when I felt his hand slowly lifting my skirt to reach between my legs. I froze up in fear and just let him touch me, but I did not enjoy it; in fact, it scared me and made me feel stupid. Of course, I wanted to tell him no, and to refuse his advances, but I was afraid of his reaction. I didn't want to seem like an uncool baby, as he was an older boy that I really liked, so I just went along with it. He didn't seem to be very worried about how I felt about it, and as he stared at the movie screen with one hand in my underwear and the other down his pants, I swore off dating for good. What good was it to me if I had to endure unwanted sexual advances and not even have fun? I declined the after-movie ice cream trip and went home instead.

My reputation as a slut snowballed after my date with

the older boy. Big boobs plus allowing an older boy to feel you up on the first date equals slut. Once you've achieved slut status, there really is no going back in teen world. Your label defines you in everything you do and some such-labeled people end up very sad about it when they're branded as whores. I wasn't. I was more angry than sad to be judged so easily, so I embraced it and freely explored my sexuality. I figured there was nothing I could ever do to change anyone's mind about rumors about me, justified or not, so there was really nothing I could do to make my reputation worse.

My slutty reputation followed me to high school and I had a bit of trouble with that my freshman year, as my reputation wasn't actually warranted. I dated boys from the senior class who expected me to put out. My sexual adventures hadn't yet taken me past mutual masturbation, so when I wouldn't have sex with guys, or even go down on them, they dumped me. While one may think I'd gain a reputation as a tease from not putting out when I was supposed to be the girl who did, I did not. Regardless of the fact that I hadn't actually slept with those guys, they told everyone they indeed scored with me, so my whorish rep remained intact.

Despite my status as school slut, I found someone who didn't care one bit what others thought of me. He saw me for whom I was inside and made me feel so amazingly loved. His name was Tony and he was my dream man in the flesh. He was tall, with dark hair and brown eyes with long black lashes, a charming smile complete with pearly white teeth, and a muscular frame with just the right amount of body fat to be considered a teddy bear sort of guy. Not only extremely attractive, he was co-captain of the football team, a lead member of our high school's drum line, and an active member of the drama club and choir. He was smart, handsome, friendly, well-liked, talented, and Italian; just the way I always pictured my dream guy. I couldn't have put together a more perfect man. I fell in love with him so fast I didn't even see it coming.

Unfortunately, there were obstacles to our love-filled romance. For one, he was a senior and I was a freshman, so he wanted to keep our relationship a secret due to the age gap (I think that was his excuse, I can't quite recall since there were so many reasons given for his need for secrecy). Second, he was young and stupid and so was I. He was stupid in the sense that he took me for granted and treated me any way he wanted to because he knew I loved him so much that I'd still give him what he wanted. I was stupid in the sense that I needed his love and affection so badly that I took everything he threw at me, no matter how bad or disrespectful, just because I loved him. He never hurt me physically- he would never, he just treated me like a whore, and I allowed it.

Tony was my first everything: first major crush, the first of several sexual experiences, and my first devastating heartbreak. Though he occasionally came home from college after he graduated high school to have sex with me, I realized doing so made me feel worse about myself and eventually stopped reaching out to him to let him use me. I had fooled myself into believing those private moments fulfilled me with a sense of love and true intimacy, but I was wrong.

I wasn't ready to date for a while after what I went through with Tony, but that didn't stop me from having sex. For me, sex was like a hobby. Though I knew I was fooling myself thinking that any of those guys really cared for me, it did make me feel special that I shared a certain intimacy with those guys that others didn't. I didn't even enjoy the sex; I enjoyed the closeness and everything else. How nice they treated me before the act, and how affectionate they were during the act. They may have been using me for something they wanted, but I was using them for something I wanted too; I just didn't know of any other way to feel the love I needed to feel, and I needed it like a drug.

CHAPTER SIXTEEN

My high school years proved to be the most difficult time in my life at home as well as in school. Everything and everyone in our household was headed in a downward spiral spinning out of control very fast.

Maddie, my once sweet, adorable, innocent little sister had turned into a black lipstick-wearing, black clothing-sporting, devil-worshipping witch of some sort who hung around scary looking people that liked to smoke weed and cast "spells" on people. She was extremely depressed, angry at the world, and antisocial and had been having some severe mental health issues that caused her to act out at home. She lashed out at everyone who dared look in her direction and had a habit of beating the crap out of anyone who tested her.

Because of Maddie's emotional and behavioral state, she was placed in a separate high school for teens with behavioral problems, which meant we were separated in school for the very first time in our lives. As twins, we'd always been in the same school, but often in separate classes. Now, we were in different schools in different towns.

David, a once happy, smiling little boy had become insecure and very timid. He was painfully shy and afraid of practically everything, and now that he was in school, he had a hard time making friends. His father was always too busy drinking with his buddies to spend any time with him, so David spent most of his time being dragged around town with Maddie and her creepy friends, out on dates with me, or at Mom-mom and Pop-pop's house watching the Home Shopping Network, golf, or playing alone in the playroom. Maddie and I had had cousins our age to spend time with when we were young, but David did not. He was a lonely child and as much as I wanted to save him from his misery, I was too held down by my own.

My mother was a tremendous nightmare during my time in high school. I'm sure she was losing it just a little bit more each and every day that Ed stumbled through the door reeking of beer and cigarettes categorically denying his drinking problem, but her hatred for Ed was displaced directly at her children every chance she got.

She'd sit at the kitchen table barking orders at Maddie, David, and me whenever she was home. She constantly craved attention and demanded it. It didn't matter what we needed or if we were in the middle of doing anything important, like schoolwork; what she needed had to be tended to now, right this moment, or the world would end.

Ed began drinking every single night and his violent outbursts had hit an all-time high. He had forgone the belt and switched to an extension cord, which he soon gave up on after I hid them all, and began hitting, slapping and punching us whenever he felt necessary. I tried to withstand the worst of the physical abuse for Maddie, but I wasn't always around. Ed didn't put his hands on David, perhaps because someone was always around or possibly because David was his own son. For Maddie and me, though, life with Ed was becoming increasingly like trying to survive a horror movie.

My mind and body ached. Unhappiness consumed me. My mental health was held intact by the thinnest of threads that threatened to break at any moment. I was floating through life just waiting for it to all fall apart. My mother's demands and need were top priority in my life and school wasn't even on my list. There were times I'd lie down to go to sleep, house neat and clean, kids fed and in bed, and my mother would come home after work and wake me up to re-hang the laundry, or re-fold towels until four in the morning when she got tired. Sometimes I'd tell myself I was just going to get some sleep until six, then get up and go to school, but then I'd awake in a panic at nine or noon and hate myself with a passion for oversleeping.

I missed so much school trying to keep up with my mother's orders. I couldn't handle school and the work that needed to be done at home, so I only went to my classes when my home life didn't prevent me from doing so. I didn't quite drop out; I just only attended the classes I liked: English, Music, and Art. My report cards were horrifying, but extremely telling of what classes I enjoyed and expended any effort in. I had straight 'F's in the classes I never attended and didn't care for and straight 'A's in English, Music, and Art.

The administrators and teachers in my school allowed this behavior from me; why, I do not know. Perhaps some of them suspected things of my home life, or perhaps they didn't really know what to do with me. I attended many meetings with guidance counselors, the principal, and the school psychologist, but I didn't trust any of them to tell them about my home life, so they really didn't know what my problem was. I felt no one could help me and that communicating my struggles would prove pointless.

The Child Study Team administered tests regarding my ability to learn by testing me for learning disabilities, but I was hardly incapable of learning, I simply didn't have the time to devote to school like most other kids in my class. The woman who tested me seemed so frustrated, as she knew I was more than capable of learning, but she couldn't get me to care about school. She didn't understand that I couldn't care. I felt bad for her because she wanted to help me so badly, but I just couldn't meet her halfway and communicate what I knew was standing in the way of my academic success.

I became especially close with my high school music teacher, Mr. Hiller, who was a very passionate person that, for some reason, believed in my ability to be a successful person. I never outright told him about my home life, but he knew something was wrong. Considering that Mr. Hiller was someone who had fought his own demons and won, he felt a responsibility to help others and share his knowledge with those who needed it. He noticed how much class I missed and looked into my personal file. His wife, Mrs. Hiller, worked in the guidance counselor's office and shared my file with him with my mother's permission. I suppose Mr. Hiller was just one of those teachers who went above and beyond for those he believed in.

When Mr. Hiller saw the pattern of my grades and how

they seemed to have fallen off at a certain point, as well as the pattern of effort I put forth in certain classes, he knew I was a smart girl and tried his very best to get me involved in the music department and keep me in school. He also helped me discover my vocal talent, which became a huge outlet for me.

Despite Mr. Hiller's efforts to help me and as much as I appreciated his support and wisdom, I wasn't ready to accept his help, nor did I feel deserving of it or able to implement it. At that time in my life, I felt my situation was out of my control and believed there was nothing I could do to fix it. Still, I took in every word he said and locked it away for later use. I still remember the most valuable thing he taught me, and though I didn't understand it fully at that time, I never forgot his lesson that, "Everything in life is a choice."

To be clear, I didn't tell people about my home life for several reasons. I didn't think it was abnormal to have it rough at home. Though I knew I had it worse than some kids did, I knew that my life could be so much worse and believed that I should appreciate what I did have instead of complaining about it. I felt I had to play the hand I was dealt. I didn't believe I could change what was already in the cards for me, especially since I believed that part of the problem was that I was inherently a bad child.

Aside from my feelings that I was helpless to change my situation, I really hated to be pitied. I didn't like it when people felt sorry for me; it was offensive to me. Even though I hated my life and struggled daily through the pain I endured at home, I felt a sense of strength at being able to survive my environment even though I wasn't truly living. I felt that people who felt sorry for me thought I was weak. I believed I wasn't weak; to me, it's a strong person who can trudge on every day through emotional and physical beatings, an unbearable weight of stress, verbal abuse, and horrible depression and still see some sort of light at the end of the tunnel.

I couldn't always be strong, despite my best efforts. I envied my classmates greatly for the privilege they had to be normal teens who worried about normal teenage things like: who was sleeping with whom, who went on class trips and saw the Empire State Building, and be concerned with and shop for the latest fashions. I wanted to be free to be young and do those things instead of taking care of a family. I wanted to go to the mall, or delve into a science project, or be on the yearbook committee. I strongly desired to be normal, but I wasn't and there was no one at all I could identify with.

Loneliness and emptiness ate away at my soul. When everything in your life is all bad and the good never stays, It's tough to remain strong and hopeful for a future that could ever possibly be like the ones you see on TV, with a happy family, a husband who loves you, a career you're good at and prepared for, and friends who truly care for you. I came to a point where I could see no hope at all for a better future and decided I could no longer take living my life anymore.

*   *   *   *   *

"Lissy, wake up!" A woman shouted at me. I felt my body being shaken, but I couldn't respond.

"Lissy, open your eyes, now! Wake up." The woman grabbed my face with one hand and sat me up with her other. I had no idea where I was. I opened my eyes and immediately closed them after the light burned my eyes.

What the hell is going on? I thought. *Am I dead?*

"Did you throw up?" The woman asked.

I shrugged and opened my eyes slowly to adjust to the bright light. She was a nurse. I was in the hospital.

"Do you know what you took?"

"No, I don't even know what's going on right now." I said, annoyed and scared.

"You overdosed on pills."

Shit. My mom's going to kill me.

"Ok, yes, I know what I took." I responded, my memory becoming clearer. "I took my sister's meds. The whole bottle. I don't have any clue how many of them there were. I believe it was Zyprexa, or Zoloft, or Xanax, but I'm not sure. Something with a 'Z' sound, I think."

"Alright, your mother is on her way and I'm going to need you to drink this- all of it." She handed me a large cup full of a thick gray substance. It looked awful.

"What is it?" I asked, practically gagging at the sight of it.

"It's charcoal. If you don't drink it, we're going to have to pump your stomach. Trust me, you don't want that."

No, I truly did not want to have my stomach pumped. I stared into the cup at the disgusting charcoal drink and frowned.

"You're alive, kid, and you're going to be whether you drink that or not, but if you don't drink it, you'll have permanent damage to other organs in your body. Now, drink it and don't purge it or we'll have to give you more." She said, and walked out of my curtained area.

I think that's what she said, anyway. I was only half-paying attention. I was too busy being disgusted by the texture of the drink in my hand. I stared at it for a few more moments, took a deep breath, and took a long chug. I attempted to swallow it without tasting it, but that didn't quite work out. I gagged at the thick texture. Why couldn't they flavor it with something? It wasn't cold or hot. It was room temperature and thick like a milkshake but with none of the flavor. It was chalky and awful. I downed the rest of it and vowed I'd never ever do anything to make myself have to drink charcoal ever again in my life.

I felt like throwing up, but I wasn't supposed to. I decided to lie down again and rest. I felt very tired. As soon as my head hit the pillow and I closed my eyes, I heard my mother's voice.

"Don't go to sleep, Lissy. Get up. Get up now and explain to me what it is that you've done."

I have no idea why I wasn't allowed to just die in peace. They had to save me and call *her*.

I sat up. "Nothing, mom. I did nothing. I just wanted to die and nobody will let me die."

"Oh your life is so terrible you have to die? I'm such a terrible mother, aren't I? Everything's always my fault. I've tried my hardest. I HAVE to work, Lissy. I have to work to put food on the table and to provide for my children. Sorry I'm such a terrible mother."

"I didn't say it was your fault."

"Then whose fault is it, Lissy? Who makes your life so bad that you want to kill yourself? Ed? Ed didn't have to be your father. He *chose* to be your father. He may not be perfect, but every day he works hard so that you and your sister and brother can have clothes, food, and a nice house and you are all ungrateful."

God, I really was ungrateful. I felt so stupid. Here I was trying to commit suicide when I had it better than so many people did. I felt so ashamed of myself. She was right. It was selfish of me to try to end my life when there were people who needed me, like her, Maddie, and David.

"How did I get here?" I asked.

"David called 9-1-1. You are so selfish; I can't even believe you would do that in front of David. He's only a little boy. You scared him to death."

Poor David, I didn't even think of that. My mother's guilt trip was really working. I felt like the crappiest person in the entire world. It hurt my heart to think I'd done something to scare him so badly. I wanted to hold him and tell him everything was ok and that I loved him. I suddenly felt glad I didn't die. I loved David and I never wanted to hurt him.

The nurse entered the room with hands full of paperwork.

"We won't be releasing you today, Miss Adams. Because of the circumstances that brought you here today, we're sending you to be evaluated at our mental health crisis center and from there, we'll decide what sort of treatment you'll need going forward." The nurse informed.

"Wait- what? You're going to send me to the loony

bin?" I asked, mortified.

"We don't call it that Miss Adams. It is likely you will be required to attend an inpatient program at a psychiatric rehabilitation facility."

No matter the fancy wording, she was sending me to the loony bin, nut house, funny farm, madhouse, whatever term you prefer. I couldn't believe it. I looked over at my mother, who had a strange look on her face. I couldn't tell whether she was trying to cry, or if she had gas. When a single tear snuck down her face, I felt like beating her in hers. I knew she was putting on a show for the nurse.

"Thank you so much for all your help, nurse." My mother said, voice dripping with honey. "I'm a nurse too. It's so sad to see young people in this situation. They just don't realize that they have their whole lives ahead of them and so much to live for. Suicide is not reversible. Oh, Lord, thank God my Lissy gets another day to live. We'll get her all the help she needs. Thank you so very much, nurse."

God, she was good. She deserved an Academy Award for that performance.

The nurse gave her the list of things I'd need and all the paperwork from our visit and we headed over to the crisis center for my psychological evaluation.

*   *   *   *   *

"Do you have thoughts of harming yourself or others?" Asked the hospital psychologist.

Yes, of course, I do, or else I wouldn't be in the hospital right now for attempted suicide! I thought.

"No." I said.

"Do you feel as though people are following you or checking on you for any reason at all?"

"Am I paranoid? No." I responded. I just wanted to go home and go to sleep. I was exhausted.

"Do you feel safe at home?"

Hell no. One day that drunk is going to kill me.

"Yes. Can I go now?"

"No, you may not. Your answers are obviously dishonest and you've just attempted suicide. I'm referring you to Washington Hospital for intensive inpatient treatment."

"How long will I have to be in there for? Months?" I was panicked at the thought of Maddie and David being alone at home with Ed without my protection. I felt sick to my stomach thinking about what would happen to them in my absence.

"It all depends on what your doctor recommends for you at the treatment facility. Your stay could be approximately one to six weeks long, depending on your level of care."

"Fine." I said, giving in. "When do I have to go to this place?"

"Now. The patient transport can take you, or your mother can take you to be admitted."

"Now? But I don't have any of my things with me, and I have to check on my sister and brother." Going away without talking to Maddie and David first seemed an impossible task.

How will they know what to do without me? I thought.

"I'm sure your mother will bring clothes for you to the facility. Let your mother worry about your siblings, and you just go take care of yourself and get better."

"I *am* better. I feel fine. I just thought I wanted to die and so I acted on it. I didn't die, so now I have to get back to life. This is crazy. I can't be away from Maddie and David. You don't understand."

"Miss Adams- Lissy, I know you feel that you're fine now, but there's a reason why you chose to attempt suicide. Though you were not successful in your attempt, the act itself tells us that you have some things going on that you need help with. We're here to make sure you're safe and emotionally healthy. Please take this opportunity to help yourself. I know you want to help your siblings, but you can't help anyone else if you're not well."

She had me there. Perhaps this would be a good thing. Maybe if I was ok, I'd be more able to help Maddie and David.

"Alright, I understand. Thank you."

"You're welcome and good luck, Lissy. I really hope things get better for you."

As I walked out of her office and into the waiting room, where my mother was chatting up a stranger, I made the decision to do the best I could in treatment, not just for me, but for Maddie and David as well.

.

CHAPTER SEVENTEEN

I arrived at the mental hospital; excuse me, psychiatric rehabilitation facility, in the middle of the night. It was a long wait while I processed in and handed over all my personal effects, including anything in my outfit that could possibly be used as a tool for suicide. Not only did they take my shoelaces, but they also took my make-up bag, which I really didn't appreciate. Apparently, the tiny mirrors in make-up compacts can be broken or removed and used to cut yourself. I wasn't a cutter so that hadn't occurred to me. It did occur to me, however, that despite all the things they took away, I still could hang myself with my sheets if I really wanted to, or drown myself in the bathroom sink. Where there's a will, there's a way.

I wasn't in there to harm myself, though. I was in there to get better, and I was excited to learn how to do that. I couldn't sleep once settled into my shared room in the juvenile ward; I was too anxious to get working on getting better and to stop having fantasies of dying. In addition, I had a roommate who snored loudly, so I couldn't sleep even if I wanted to.

A few hours after I had arrived, it was time for breakfast. We were brought breakfast trays that seemed to have been sitting out for hours, so I gave mine to my roomie, who was on some heavy meds that made her constantly ravenous. We were served in a solarium that looked straight out of a movie set. The color scheme was various shades of outdated green and an ugly pale yellow. The windows weren't glass, either. They were some thick pliable material with handprints all over them. You could almost read the invisible finger-painted "help me" message in between the smudges. It was depressing and felt dirty.

Looking around the room, I noticed that nobody really looked sick. I only saw two people there who appeared to fit the stereotype of the mentally ill patient: one who believed himself to be Satan, and the other, Satan's wife. I'm not sure if they came in together, or if they had met while both being patients, but they definitely seemed to be happy, or… something, together.

It was extremely clear to me that day that there really is no specific look of mental illness. Any one of those kids could walk past me on the street and I'd never once think they were suffering from depression, substance abuse, schizophrenia, bipolar, or an eating disorder. Mental illness has no face; it simply looks the same as "normal". When you see a mentally ill person on TV, it's an extreme caricature; in real life, they look no different from you.

Still, my beliefs about what it meant to have a mental illness made me feel as if I did not belong and shouldn't be there. I felt, probably like most other people who were there, that I didn't belong there because I wasn't that bad and that my problems were not as serious as others' were. I did think attempted suicide was a serious issue, but I felt my attempt was justified and that there wasn't really a way I could be helped because nobody could change my situation. I felt others could be helped because medication could treat them. How could talking about things change my situation? I didn't believe it could.

After breakfast, we had a full schedule of group therapies and activities for the day. Half of the group sessions didn't apply to me because they were all based on substance abuse, so I didn't have to attend them. Instead, I sat around drawing or writing while other people went to the meetings. When it was time for a group that did relate to me, I attended but didn't speak except when spoken to. I didn't feel comfortable speaking in front of a group.

Mental illness didn't have a face, but it sure had a voice. I couldn't tell which specific mental illness belonged to which person, but those who believed they were of grand importance dominated the speaking time in group therapy. They spoke loudly and dramatically and were prone to cutting off other people as they spoke. I had no patience for those people. Although I knew they couldn't control the behaviors caused by their illness, it prevented me from speaking up because I had a hard enough time doing so, and to be cut off made me feel like my feelings weren't important, so I kept my mouth shut.

Since group therapy wasn't very effective for me, I wasn't making much progress during my stay. They had put me on some medication, but I needed one on one treatment. I was a private person, on top of being more of a listener than a speaker, in group settings. By my second week at the hospital, my care manager noticed this, and I was given some individual therapy on a daily basis.

My individual therapy sessions were probably the least helpful experiences in my entire life because my mother attended them with me; possibly because I was a minor, or maybe because my therapist didn't pay one shred of attention to me at all when I spoke. Either way, my manipulative mother turned my therapist against me and convinced him that I was an ungrateful brat who was melodramatic and exaggerating how badly I had it at home.

She claimed I was physically punished only as a form of discipline. She pointed to various socioeconomic reasons to support her claim: our nice home, their financially comfortable situation that allowed me luxuries other kids didn't have, her level of education and professional job in the medical field as a nurse, Ed's honorable and humble jobs as farmer and firefighter. Because my life sounded so good on paper, I had no logical reason to be depressed or to attempt suicide. She claimed I attempted suicide for attention; my therapist agreed with her.

I felt tremendously betrayed by my therapist, a person who was supposed to be there to help me. Surely, suicide attempts can be "for attention" but that doesn't exclude them from also being, at the same time, cries for help. I began questioning the helpfulness of the mental health system concerning juveniles. If my abuser was required to attend therapy with me, how honest could I be in an environment regarded as "safe" but was, in reality, only temporary and at the end, I had to return to an environment that, in my opinion, was unsafe? I couldn't be honest. Long-term, I had no protection from the things I divulged in therapy; once my stay in the hospital was over, I'd go back home and pay for the ways I spoke against my family.

I decided not to say another word while in the hospital,

as I felt it was pointless. I allowed my mother to dominate my therapy sessions for the rest of my stay and when I was eventually released after three weeks of "treatment", I only felt more helpless than I had before I'd been admitted.

*   *   *   *   *

Following my stay in the mental hospital, I was more depressed than I'd ever been in my entire life. The only solace I found in my daily life was that one day soon, I'd turn eighteen and be free to leave home for good. I vowed to take Maddie and David and cut off all contact from my family for good.

Looking for ways to fill my time productively until my eighteenth birthday, I got my first job outside of my summer work on the family farm at a fast food restaurant. Since I was only sixteen, I required working papers signed by my mother in order to be able to take the job. Since she knew I really wanted the job, she refused to sign my working papers for a few weeks until finally giving in.

I was thrilled to be working and earning a paycheck. I had plans to save up all my money for a place to live for my siblings and myself. Making minimum wage, I didn't earn much, so I worked overtime and any extra shifts available to me. I would go to school, then straight to work, and Pop-pop would pick me up in the evenings, or I'd hang around until eleven at night until my mother got off work. I hated to have Ed pick me up drunk. He'd try to talk to my co-workers and I didn't like people to know my business. Work was a great escape for me and I didn't want my home life mixed with my work life in any sense.

My plans to hoard my money were thwarted when my

104

mother suddenly demanded I pay her rent. My savings were barely mounting up to anything as it was, but she demanded $500 per month in rent. If I worked extra shifts, I was lucky to bring home $600 per month, so her request for rent payments set my plans back greatly. Being left with only $100 per month meant I had nothing left over to save, and I was working hard to pay to live in a place I'd have gladly escaped at a moment's notice.

I was only sixteen years old and there were hardly any good-paying jobs for minors without a high school diploma, and I couldn't save anything if my mother required me to pay rent if I had a job. My solution to the situation was to get rid of my job. Why work myself to death if I couldn't get ahead?

The sense of pride and independence I'd gained from having had a job diminished after I quit. I felt lost with no direction and no one to help me see a way out of my hopeless situation. I believed that turning eighteen and getting a high school diploma was my final hope; I'd simply have to cope however I could with the misery in my life until that day came.

CHAPTER EIGHTEEN

As a sixteen year-old, my knowledge of how to cope with stress and depression was lacking quite a bit. Healthy coping skills like eating right, sleeping right, and avoiding stressful situations were impossible for me to implement because I could never sleep in peace at home, eat on a schedule, and my whole life was a stressful situation in which every single day I had to fight like hell to survive a house of total madness.

I coped by dropping out of school and smoking weed, marijuana, herb, bud, whatever you want to call it. My friend Jessa introduced me to this wonderful plant, which became something I relied upon to feel good and to lessen my emotional pain. Weed calmed me down and made dealing with my home life much easier thanks to its euphoria-inducing and inhibition-lowering characteristics.

Though I realized I was self-medicating my emotional pain, I found weed to be a helpful tool to use to think more objectively about my problems at home and to think of realistic plans for my future free from emotional obstacles. I enjoyed the ability to escape my sadness, feel peace, and be able to relax through smoking. Though I knew marijuana was illegal, I believed it to be much less harmful than drinking alcohol, as I had never seen anyone smoke weed and beat up their wife or children, but I had seen with my own eyes the aggression and violence that often occurred under the influence of alcohol.

I flirted with some other drugs as well, but I can't really say weed was a gateway drug for me because I would have tried other drugs regardless whether or not weed existed in this world as long as there was a chance of relief from my emotional suffering. Though marijuana was an everyday "drug" I could use to cope with life, I found a recreational drug that took away every worry I had in the world-Ecstasy.

*   *   *   *   *

"I got some pills from CJ that he says we absolutely have to try!" Jessa said, excitedly, entering her bedroom and plopping down on her bed.

CJ was an acquaintance of ours who sold us weed. He was extremely unattractive and not very socially adept, but always had good stuff.

"What are they?" I asked, curious.

"E-pills. Ecstasy, they call it. They're supposed to make you outrageously happy and feel amazingly good."

She had me at "outrageously happy." I didn't question her further.

"When are we doing this?"

I was staying the night at Jessa's house, and we had planned to lounge around in our pajamas, do each other's hair and make-up, and eat a whole roll of cookie dough that night.

"Tonight. CJ's having a party at his house and a bunch of us are going to roll together."

"Roll?"

"It's what it's called when you do E. You roll, or like you are rolling on E." She informed.

"Oh. Ew. Makes me think of eyes rolling in the back of your head or something."

"I know, ew! Yeah, that only happens to people who take more than one pill. They get too high and get sloppy. We're not doing that. That's gross."

"Alright, sounds good. Let's get ready! I hope some hot guys will be there!" I said.

"Me too! Uh!" She giggled and hopped up off her bed to raid her closet while I got our make-up and curling irons set up. We were going to look fabulous for this party!

When we got to the party, there was a bunch of guys there. One guy in particular caught my eye with his bleached spiky hair, dark roots, and sexy eyes.

"Who is that?" I asked Jessa, my heart in my throat. He was extremely hot. So much so that I was too nervous to even think around him.

"Oh that's Jackson. He's taken, unfortunately. I know. He's hot, right?" She said, with a look of disappointment on her face. Obviously, I wasn't the only one who had immediately crushed on him.

"Oh my gosh! Yes! Let's move away from him. His hotness is affecting my ability to breathe." I said, and spun around in a direction away from the off-limits eye candy.

We settled down on the couch near the TV where some friend-zone guys were sitting and prepared to take our pills. We decided to take them at the same time and promised to look out for each other. I loved Jessa and would never let anything happen to her. I knew I could trust her to have my back too.

"You'll start to feel it in about half an hour." She told me. "Drink lots of water and stay hydrated. Don't drink alcohol or smoke weed, just enjoy this pill, ok? Trust me."

"Ok, I'll drink lots of water and not do anything but this. I do trust you. Love you!"

"Love you too, bitch. Cheers!"

"Cheers!"

We clinked our water bottles together and swallowed our pills at the same time.

As we waited for our pills to kick in, other people began to arrive at the party. A few more guys and one girl sat at the dining room table in the dining room, which was essentially the same room as the living room in the small apartment. We could see them from where we were sitting on the couch and I zeroed in on one person immediately.

"Do you see that tall guy with the dark hair and the red hat?" Jessa asked, pointing at him.

"Yeah, he's cute." His eyes met mine as he noticed us looking at him. Quickly looking away, he resumed setting up the card game the guys were about to have at the dining room table.

"Yeah, he is. He's Jackson's little brother Jacob."

"Oh, they are both hot!"

"The Wilson brothers are all hot. There are three of them: Jackson, Jacob, and the other one is Jordan. They're all in relationships, except for the youngest one- Jacob."

"Oh, ok. How old is Jacob?" I knew Jackson was a couple years older than Jessa and I, so I figured Jacob had to be our age.

"He's a year younger than us," she said, frowning, "but he's really mature for his age."

I personally didn't care about his age. He was handsome and mysterious and had an air about him that was innocent and pure. I snuck glances at him frequently and caught him looking at me a few times.

"So, do you have a thing for him, or can I go talk to him?" I asked.

"No, no, go ahead. I have my eye on the blonde boy who's shuffling the cards like a casino dealer. You know blondes are my thing!" She said with a giggle, eyeing him up.

"Ok, I'll talk to Jacob, but not right this second. I'm pretty sure my pill is kicking in."

"I think mine is too." She said smiling.

I was a little nervous to feel the pill's effects. I wasn't sure what to expect and I had begun sweating and clenching my jaw. It was making me nervous that I was grinding my teeth so hard. A few moments later, though, I felt warmth in my body that seemed to spread from my core and outward to my extremities. A warm, delicious, beautiful happiness swept over me and I felt so much euphoria that nothing could have felt better to me at that moment than just being in my own skin under the effects of Ecstasy.

I sunk into the comfy couch and sighed a deep sigh, which felt amazing, took a sip of water, which tasted delicious, and smoked a cigarette, which felt incredible to inhale. My senses were magnified to a degree I had never experienced.

"I believe I'm going to vomit." I said unusually calmly and cheerfully to Jessa.

"Ok, do you want me to come with you and hold your hair?" She asked softly with an exaggerated amount of compassion.

"No, it's ok but thank you very much. I love you so much." I said, floating on my Ecstasy cloud of butterflies and unicorns.

"Love you too, Lissy. You're my best friend in the whole world." She said as she closed her eyes and caressed the couch with her fingertips.

Making my way to the bathroom, I passed Jacob, who stopped me and asked me if I was ok.

"I'm alright and you're gorgeous, but I have to throw up I think, so I'm going to the bathroom." I said, touching his cheek in admiration of his handsomeness.

I had no filter from brain to mouth and everything I said just sounded so easy and right. I made my way to the bathroom and as I was closing the door, Jacob stuck his head in.

"Please let me help you. You will feel much better after you throw up. Is this your first time?" He asked.

"Your eyelashes look like butterflies and they're beautiful, but your eyes might fly away. I don't know what I'm talking about. You can help me, but I'm going to throw up and I'm sure you don't want to see that so-". I vomited.

It was the easiest vomiting experience I've ever had- no retching, just a quick release, then an awesomely high feeling. Jacob had acted quickly and gathered my hair away from my face. When I was done, he released my hair and got me a cool wet paper towel to wipe my face, then handed me my water bottle so I could rinse out my mouth.

"Thank you, Jacob. You're so sweet and kind. I love that you just took care of me. That's so attractive and you're a super-hot angel with arms like a lumberjack." My words were sickeningly cheesy, and I couldn't stop saying weird things.

I looked him in his deep brown eyes framed with long black lashes and saw into his soul; it was breathtaking. He was so beautiful, inside and out, and at that very moment, I knew I loved him. With every shred of my being, I felt a love I had never felt before in my entire life. It was a love that couldn't be explained in words, but could be communicated with just one look.

He grabbed me around my waist and pulled my body tightly to his, holding me in his strong arms. I responded by wrapping my arms around his neck and, standing on my toes to meet his height, snuggling my face into his neck. It felt right, almost as if I had arrived home after being gone for years. It was a love that I couldn't explain or understand, yet it was there, and we both felt it. It was beyond sexual, which was certainly different for me given my past endeavors.

We stood holding each other for quite a long time saying nothing, but reveling in heightened emotions. When we finally released our hold on each other, we were breathless as if we had made out wildly, yet our lips hadn't even touched. We joined the rest of the party where everyone else was in deep conversation about how amazing each other were and never once took our eyes off one another.

It didn't occur to me in the midst of my drug-fueled high that my feelings for Jacob may have been solely due to the effects of the drug. I enjoyed the night feeling loved completely and truly by someone who knew nothing about me, and I felt the greatest love I've ever felt for someone I knew equally as little about.

When we finally came down from our high, we fell asleep on the floor of CJ's apartment holding each other; my head in his chest and his arms wrapped around me tightly. Though I hadn't wanted the intense euphoria of the night to end, I was excited to spend the next day with Jacob outside the veil of Ecstasy.

CHAPTER NINETEEN

In the sobering light of day, Jacob and I discovered that the love we felt the night before had indeed had some basis in reality. Though our drug high had passed, we were still high on our unexplainable magnetic attraction to each other. We spent the entire day together after that night just talking and walking around the town where CJ lived. We discovered that we had a lot in common, including a less than traditional family life. Jacob and I understood each other and took solace in the unconditional acceptance and friendship we offered one another.

After that first night together, Jacob and I were inseparable and fell deeply and passionately in love. I can't recall ever having known someone who loved me endlessly without judgment and truly without conditions aside from my grandparents. Jacob cared for me as though I were something valuable, something precious. With him, I never questioned that he thought I was the most beautiful, intelligent, perfect person in the world for him, and he showed me true love in so many ways.

Above all, Jacob taught me how to love myself, which was probably one of the most valuable lessons I learned in life. He never let me doubt myself and always encouraged me to do the right things for myself, no matter his own personal feelings. My relationship with Jacob inspired me in my own life. He taught me that I was indeed a person who deserved to be loved and treated with respect; therefore, I demanded nothing less from those in my life. He made me believe I wasn't a bad person and that I indeed had wonderful qualities. As a result, I began to give myself a bit more credit for my positive traits. His love made me feel beautiful and as if I could accomplish anything in life, and I began to believe I could achieve the things I dreamed of achieving.

Jacob's brothers, Jackson and Jordan, had gone through some struggles in their youth and made out successfully as adults, which made them a great example for Jacob and me because they held jobs, had loving relationships, and were both in the process of creating families of their own. I wasn't particularly close with Jackson or Jordan, but I admired them greatly and saw through their lives the potential for happiness for Jacob and me.

My relationship with Jacob was an amazing journey. We loved each other dearly, we could talk about anything, and we handled conflict together productively and effectively. We fought, like all other couples, but never to the level that my mother and Ed reached in their fights. Jacob was compassionate and caring and put me first. I knew he was the only one for me, and, in my eyes, nobody could ever measure up to Jacob.

Our relationship took quite the serious turn when one night, in the midst of our passion, we had forgone using protection during lovemaking. As often happens in nature, I became pregnant.

"Jacob, I have to tell you something." I said hesitantly. I had gone to his house to tell him face to face as soon as I found out.

"Hey, baby. What is it?" He said, giving me a hug and a kiss as I entered his apartment.

I sat down on the couch, hugging my purse to my chest.

"I'm pregnant."

At sixteen, I thought.

The look on his face was pensive.

"Are you sure?" He asked.

"Well, my period is more than a week late and I took three home pregnancy tests that were positive, so yes I'm fairly certain."

He wasn't upset or angry, so I took that as a good sign.

"That's awesome!" His face lit up and his warm smile washed calmness over me.

"Phew! I wasn't sure what you'd say. I was so nervous to tell you. Obviously we knew there was a chance this would happen after that one night."

"Yes, we knew. We kind of just left it up to God." Jacob was a very spiritual person. I admired that about him; I wished I could believe in a loving heavenly father in the sky who cared for you when no one else did.

"Yes. So we're going to keep it then?" I asked.

"Of course we are!" He sounded a bit offended that I'd suggest anything else. "This is our child, made from our love."

"Well, when you put it like that, it sounds beautiful." I smiled.

Wrapping me in his arms, he put his hand on my chin and lifted my face to meet his. Looking me in the eyes, he said matter-of-factly, "It is."

*   *   *   *   *

I wasn't as convinced as Jacob was that having a baby was a beautiful thing. Sure, it *sounded* amazing the way he put it, but when considering that he and I were only teenagers, fifteen and sixteen, respectively, it seemed so un-amazing. Of course, I had envisioned us getting married and having children together in the future, but in that fantasy, I had envisioned finishing high school and going to college first.

I knew I should not have allowed myself to get pregnant, because, let's be real, that's what happened; there were many birth control methods we could have used, but we made a lust-filled decision not to utilize any method, and now we had to face the consequences of that decision and take responsibility for it. Despite my age, lack of education, and lack of finances, I loved my baby the moment I knew it was growing inside me. The fact that my baby was a child born from true love and someone I loved so deeply made it impossible for me not to want to bring the child into this world.

Jacob and I began making plans for our future and trying to scrape together some sort of life for our future child and us. My friend Osenia, who had birthed a child at a young age and was quite motherly to me, guided me through what to expect and gave Jacob and me a temporary place to live together while we saved money for our own place. She was supportive of our decision to bring our child into the world and did whatever she could to help.

Not everyone was as supportive of my pregnancy, which I understood at my young age. My friends, though they had wanted to see me get an education and a career I loved before having children, supported me; Mom-mom and Pop-pop did as well. My parents were adamantly against my pregnancy, but I believe their lack of support was less about wanting better for me, and more about enjoying the sight of me in a vulnerable situation.

*   *   *   *   *

The day of my move from my parents' home to Osenia's apartment, my parents sat in the living room watching me carry my things out of the house. As I carried the last load of boxes to Osenia's waiting car, I overheard my parents making snide remarks about Jacob and my unborn child. It wasn't difficult to hear them; they were intentionally speaking loud enough for me to hear.

"That baby is going to be deformed!" Ed said with a hearty laugh.

"I know!" My mother agreed. "With all the drugs that drug addict does, that kid is going to come out with an arm growing out of its forehead."

My heart ached for the child inside me as they continued laughing at its expense. I vowed never to subject him or her to them.

"Can you imagine what kind of horror it's going to look like? It'll probably be retarded." My mother was really having a fabulous time entertaining Ed with her vile comments.

I couldn't hold my tongue.

"You two are fucking disgusting. You sit there bad-mouthing Jacob, calling him a drug addict when neither of you have any room to judge and you're calling my child mutant devil spawn, or whatever it is you're saying. You are the worst parents ever. I feel sorry that Maddie and David are stuck here with you two. You're both pure evil."

They burst out into laughter as I walked out the door in tears.

CHAPTER TWENTY

Moving in with Osenia was a very big change for me in that I had never lived away from home, nor had I ever lived with a boyfriend. I struggled with the guilt of leaving Maddie and David to be with Ed and my mother alone and worried daily about their safety, wondering constantly whether they would be ok without me there to protect them. Though I knew I should focus on my new life with Jacob and the family we were about to start together, I had left Maddie and David on their own entirely and it hurt my heart terribly to leave them behind.

Living with a boyfriend for the first time was certainly new and required a great amount of adjustment for the both of us; suddenly we had gone from teenagers having fun and smoking weed, to expectant parents looking for jobs and apartments. It was a big responsibility to step up to, and being quite young and immature proved to make our relationship tumultuous.

Soon after our move, our fairytale love began to slowly fall apart. Though Jacob had found a job doing landscaping and I had begun working at the local hospital as a nurse's aide, we weren't quite working out as a couple. Jacob began disappearing for hours and sometimes days and missing work, which made me question not only his faithfulness, but also his dependability. With the breakdown of communication and trust between us, I worried whether or not my child would have a reliable father in his or her life.

I spent many nights crying to Osenia wondering what was going on with Jacob and to where he was regularly disappearing. He would take the bus to his parents' house about an hour away and, for reasons unknown to me, would keep missing the bus back to Arbor Falls. I wasn't sure what he was up to when he disappeared, but I begged him to tell me. He insisted nothing was going on, but I knew in my heart that he wasn't being truthful. I believed wholeheartedly he was cheating on me.

Even though Jacob would disappear at times, he'd always come back, make it up to me, and apologize, then we'd make up and I'd forget all about the fact that I'd been an emotional wreck for days wondering where he was. I always said I was going to end things when he returned, but Jacob knew how to reel me back in easily. Our relationship mimicked that of my mother and Ed's in that Jacob would hurt me and the next day we'd act as if nothing had happened and be right back in the honeymoon phase, an unhealthy cycle I did not want to continue, but couldn't seem to end.

The last time Jacob disappeared, Osenia, as my friend, felt it was time to have a chat with me about the love of my life and father of my child.

"Lissy, we need to talk." Osenia stated with a tone of

concern.

She sat me down in the living room and handed me a cold can of Pepsi, my favorite drink. I knew it was going to be bad if she was trying to give me something to cheer me up before we even got started.

"Ok. What is it?" I asked nervously, clutching my can of soda tightly.

She pulled out an orange prescription bottle and shook it to show me it was empty.

"I don't understand." I said, confused.

"This bottle was hidden in my drawer. Like, hidden really well behind some clothes and books in my dresser drawer. It was a bottle of Percocet. I had hidden it so my kids didn't accidentally find it. I've had this bottle for two years and there were several pills left. I only take them when I get migraines. I went to take one yesterday and found the bottle in my drawer empty."

She searched my face for understanding. I wasn't getting what this had to do with me.

"Lissy, I believe Jacob took my pills." She said straight out.

I was at a loss for words.

Why would Jacob take her pills? Did he go through her drawers? That's highly inappropriate. No, that can't be.

"Are you sure nobody else took them?" I asked, hoping there was a possibility someone else had gotten into her stash.

"I'm sure. I haven't had anyone else here. That's not all I wanted to talk about though," she said, inhaling deeply and taking great pains to soften the blow of her words, "I think Jacob has been disappearing to do drugs behind your back."

"What? Drugs? Like what- Heroin or something? Why do you think that?"

I was in complete shock. It hadn't occurred to me that that was even a possible explanation. I had thought he was spending time with another girl. I knew something was going on, considering his habit of going missing and the fact that his stories never added up. I knew he was hiding something, I just didn't know what.

"I honestly don't know what drugs he's doing, but I know he's addicted to something and I know he took my pills. Honestly, I am not judging him, but I can't have him in my house if he's going through my private things. I don't trust him and my kids live here. I can't put them at risk."

"No, I totally understand, I just can't believe that he would go through your things. I feel like a fool. How stupid can I be? I don't even realize he's on drugs?" I felt like crying, but the tears wouldn't come.

"I'm so sorry, Lissy. I want you to be happy, and I want the best for you and your child. You know I'll always help you any way I can, and you are welcome to stay here, but he needs to go live with his parents or go to rehab. You two are expecting a child together and that child needs a father who can be an adult and provide." She hugged me tightly and retreated to the kitchen.

I just sat there with both arms wrapped around my belly feeling naïve. My child deserved better than this. I always dreamed that if I ever had children, they'd never have to grow up with a father like Ed. I had let them down before they even entered this world.

*   *   *   *   *

"Hey babe, I'm heading back from my parents' house now." Jacob said over the payphone at the bus station.

"Ok, so when will you get here?" I asked.

"Probably in about two hours." He replied.

"Alright, see you then." I said, hanging up the phone.

Osenia had agreed to let him stay one more night so I could talk to him about everything we had discussed and so that he and I would have the opportunity to discuss our options as a couple going forward.

I waited up for Jacob that night well past the time he said he'd arrive. At around ten o'clock that night, I began to doze off while watching TV. I had been having some stomach cramps since eating dinner and wanted to go to sleep after not being able to find any relief. Pregnancy prevented me from taking anything for relief; I was always too afraid to hurt my baby.

Not long after I fell asleep on the couch, I heard knocking on the front door; it was Jacob. I looked at the clock, which read somewhere around midnight, and shuffled sleepily to the door to let him in.

"Hey baby." He said, attempting to hug me, but getting his fingers caught in my messy hair, accidentally pulling it roughly.

"Ouch!" I said, disentangling him from my hair and turning away from him. "You're very late. I fell asleep."

"Yeah, I'm sorry. I missed the bus, then I saw my buddy and he waited with me for the next one, but we got talking and I missed that one too so he gave me a ride." He lied.

"Oh ok." I pretended to believe. His pupils were pinpoints. I didn't know what that meant, but I knew it wasn't normal. We made our way into the living room, where we "lived" and plopped down on separate couches.

"My stomach hurts. I think I'm going to go to back to sleep. Do you work tomorrow?" I asked.

"Ok, I'm going to take a shower and watch TV. No, I don't work tomorrow, do you?"

"No. I need to talk to you tomorrow about something important, ok? Just not right now. I don't feel well." I said, rolling over on the couch, facing away from him. I covered myself with my blanket and closed my eyes. I didn't feel like talking; all I wanted was to go back to sleep.

"Ok. I hope you feel better. What do you want to talk about? Is everything ok?" He asked.

"Yes, I just need to talk, but not now." I said, and dozed off into a deep sleep.

*   *   *   *   *

I woke up at around six o'clock in the morning feeling as if I had to move my bowels with extreme urgency. Osenia was getting ready for work in the bathroom and I banged on the door loudly.

"Osenia! Please! I have to go to the bathroom. It's an emergency!" I shouted desperately.

"Ok, ok, calm down!" She said, opening the door.

I didn't wait for her to exit. I pulled my underwear down and sat on the toilet to go. Only I hadn't had to move my bowels; the cramps, though they had felt like it, were not from an upset stomach.

"Oh my God!" I said, panicked. "Osenia, come here quick!" I noticed I had blood spots on my underwear and looked into the toilet beneath me and saw nothing but red.

"I'm right here, Lissy. You're bleeding. Just stay right there and calm down." She said, trying to maintain her composure.

"Did I have a miscarriage?" I asked her, feeling faint. "I can't look! Is my baby in the toilet? Oh my God!" I was beyond freaked out. "Don't flush the toilet!"

"Lissy, I'm so sorry, let me look. Just breathe and try to calm down as much as you possibly can." She said, with sorrow and compassion in her voice. She helped me stand up and looked in the toilet to check for a fetus. Osenia was definitely a true friend.

"I'm not sure if you've had a miscarriage or not. I don't see a fetus, but there's a lot of blood. Let me get Jacob up and we'll get you to the hospital and find out what's going on." Osenia was the only thing holding me somewhat together.

"Please don't flush my baby down the toilet!" I screamed. I was hysterical. "If it's in there, I want to get it out and bury it!"

Osenia left me in the bathroom for a moment and got Jacob from the living room. He came into the bathroom looking panicked and startled. With tears in his eyes, he helped me to clean up and dress for the trip to the hospital; I cried the entire way there.

*   *   *   *   *

At the hospital, the doctors informed me that I had had a "Spontaneous Abortion," the medical term for a miscarriage. They said it was a "complete abortion," which meant that I had indeed passed all fetal material and would not need any medical procedures as a result. I was early in my pregnancy, only twelve weeks along, and, according to the doctor, it wasn't uncommon for miscarriage to occur during that time.

All that truly registered with me was that I had indeed lost my baby in the toilet, which had to be flushed despite my pleas because Osenia's children lived in the apartment, and it was best not to traumatize them by allowing them to happen upon a toilet full of blood. I was devastated by the thought that my baby was flushed down the toilet and had horrible visions of the scene replaying in my mind for quite a long time afterward.

The loss of my child left me in a state of emotional numbness, almost as if I hurt so immensely, I couldn't feel a thing. I couldn't eat, sleep, work, shower, or function like a normal person. I lost my job and my will to get out of bed. Though I hadn't gotten a chance to have "the talk" with Jacob as I was supposed to, Osenia understood my emotional fragility and handled it for me. She asked Jacob to stay with his parents while I took some time alone to heal.

Jacob and I kept in touch over the phone while living separately, but I felt so devastated by everything that had happened, I couldn't be there for Jacob as a girlfriend, and he didn't seem to realize that I needed someone to be there for me. Osenia cared for me while I was emotionally broken. She was an amazing friend and wonderful support for me during my darkest times. She understood things about what I was going through that I didn't even understand myself; and, when I finally felt ready and able to, she helped me gain the strength to break things off with Jacob.

I'm not sure exactly what I said to Jacob when I ended our relationship, but I know it was a very abrupt and finite break; I informed him that our relationship was over, and then refused his calls. I couldn't discuss breaking up with him because we had been down that road before and he knew how to talk me out of it. He always promised to change and would repeatedly swear to me he'd never hurt me again. I always took him back, but this time, I couldn't.

For me, loving Jacob wasn't enough of a reason to continue our relationship. It turned out; Jacob was indeed addicted to drugs (prescription painkillers to be exact), which he admitted to me after my miscarriage. His admission came as a result of the guilt he felt over possibly being the cause of our lost child, which I assured him was probably not the case considering the commonality of miscarriage in the early weeks of pregnancy, as well as the level of stress I had been under during my pregnancy.

Jacob's addiction alone wasn't enough for me to leave his side; loving an addict is an extremely difficult thing. It's extremely consuming, in that the needs of the addict come first. Personally, I questioned what part I played in his addiction and poured over what responsibility I had in causing his addiction. Had I done something to make him to turn to drugs? I felt immensely guilty, but also very hurt because I didn't understand addiction and I couldn't comprehend why he couldn't just go to rehab and stop doing drugs. I couldn't understand why our love wasn't enough to make him stop abusing pills.

Before Jacob finally admitted to me that he had been abusing drugs, the lies he told to hide his addiction had already worn me down greatly. Anyone who has ever been cheated on and lied to constantly about it can understand how crazy I felt when I'd ask Jacob if he was up to something. He'd vehemently deny doing anything wrong behind my back, and become offended that I'd even think such a thing. I felt lost and didn't know what to believe; my gut told me I was right, but Jacob told me I was wrong. I had no proof of any wrongdoing, aside from his hours spent missing, so I felt foolish and paranoid thinking such things about him.

Walking away from Jacob was one of the hardest things I've ever had to do in my life, but I knew it was the best thing for me to do for myself. Jacob's actions left me in a constant state of worry; it was extremely unhealthy for me to be in a relationship with him. I needed to heal from all the hurt and pain I had experienced, and unfortunately, Jacob was part of the hurt I had to leave behind. What scared me the most about leaving Jacob was that cutting off the bad also meant sacrificing the good; to give up on my relationship meant surrendering the love I desperately wanted and needed. I had to walk away from our relationship for my own emotional health and sanity. I had two choices: stay in "love" and remain in pain, or be alone, lose my "love" and take care of me.

I chose me.

CHAPTER TWENTY-ONE

After leaving Jacob, I was glued to Osenia's living room floor for three days sobbing endlessly and basking in depressive thoughts. Osenia tried desperately to get me to participate in life, but I couldn't; I didn't want to live anymore. I felt that if I slept enough, I could possibly just sleep myself into death, a daydream that I spent an excessive amount of time replaying in my mind. I didn't want to struggle anymore and life always seemed to be such a difficult thing for me to handle. I was at the point where I believed there was no chance for happiness for me.

Following a few days of waking up in the middle of the night watching infomercials and falling asleep mid-day to old episodes of The Maury Show, I decided to force myself to pretend to be emotionally capable enough to rejoin the world. I figured if I couldn't be a normal person naturally, I could just adhere to the old adage, "Fake it 'til you make it," and pretend to be a mentally healthy person until I tricked myself into being one.

To my surprise, this actually worked for me; forcing

myself to do everyday things like showering, brushing my teeth, and facing the world, despite depression's attempts to keep me in bed, my depression began to fade. Feeling better caused me to perform more actions to improve my own happiness, like finding a new job, and doing things to make myself feel better. Finding a new job gave me independence and confidence, and I began to spend my time and energy taking care of other people.

The rewarding nature of my job as a Nursing Assistant in a nursing home allowed me to feel that I had a purpose in my life other than being someone's daughter, sister, or girlfriend. I loved caring for the residents of the home, and although I had to deal with the loss of several residents I became close with, knowing I had made the last few months, weeks, days, or hours of their lives more comfortable and positive made me feel that I had something valuable to offer the world.

Having Osenia's support helped too, and she served not only as a true friend, but also as a testament to what it meant to be a strong, independent woman. Osenia had overcome much of the same abuse I had endured in my life, but also had gone in and out of foster homes most of her life. She had her first child at the age of fifteen and was left to raise her daughter as a single mother. Still, she pressed on and always tried to make her life better through good choices. She got her high school diploma, got a job, and provided for her daughter and herself with the help and support of close friends. Osenia taught me that not only can a person choose a better life despite their circumstances, but that they can also create their own family from great friends.

When I felt strong enough to try to make it on my own without Osenia's daily guidance, she introduced me her friend Maggie, a woman who had been a crucial element to her own success as an adult. Maggie was a cheerful, sensitive, married mother of two adult children. She was my mother's age and had a huge heart and a habit of taking in stray teenagers; she provided them with the loving, accepting environment they needed, and she was rewarded by seeing them flourish as a result of her own investment in them. Her selflessness paid off more often than not, and when she agreed to take me in, I hoped her investment in me would pay off.

*   *   *   *   *

Maggie was a mystery to me. I moved in with her, accepted her help, and appreciated it greatly, but due to my own personal issues with an inability to trust others, I had a hard time believing her help came with no strings attached. She didn't want me to pay rent, clean for her, cook for her, or do anything for her, yet she provided me with a free furnished bedroom and a ride to and from work every day. I didn't understand why she cared about me. What did she have to gain from helping me? I gave her nothing, so I didn't understand why she gave so much to me. I felt I didn't deserve this blessing when I had done nothing to earn it. I suppose I wasn't trusting of her kindness because I hadn't ever been given anything before without someone expecting something in return.

It felt so wrong to me to be accepting Maggie's help without giving something in return that I began feeling extremely guilty living at her house rent-free and felt a strong desire to leave. Instead of acting on that impulse, I wrote her a letter telling her how I felt and explained my feelings to her; I preferred to write my feelings to people rather than speak them because I wasn't particularly skilled in the art of conversation, especially when it had to do with my feelings. It wasn't that I didn't know what to say or how I felt; it was just that I usually couldn't talk about my feelings without losing control of my emotions. Writing letters to people allowed me to say what I needed to say without crying or yelling.

I handed Maggie the note one day as she was dropping me off at work for the evening shift. She promised me she would read it while I was at work, and we could talk about it when she picked me up that night after my shift ended.

At work that day, I was very nervous to hear Maggie's reaction to my letter. I spent the entire eight-hour shift worried that she'd be angry that I questioned her sincerity, or hurt that I had thought she might be like every other adult in my life that had let me down. Time flew by fast as I dreaded the ride home with Maggie; I was convinced I'd be looking for a place to live tonight after she kicked me out of her house for questioning her motives.

After checking on all my residents and clocking out that night, I headed outside to smoke a cigarette while I waited for Maggie to arrive.

Just as I lit my cigarette, I saw Maggie pull up.

Damn it! What a waste. I thought. Maggie didn't smoke, so I had to put out my freshly lit cancer stick.

Maggie rolled down the passenger side window. "It's ok, kid. Finish it. I'm just going to read this one chapter of my book. I've been trying to read it all day!" She was so nice, and if I didn't know how much she loved to read and sneak a chapter in every chance she got, I would have put my cigarette out and got in the car.

As I puffed, I watched her happily devouring her book, face in deep concentration as she struggled to read the words by the dim interior light of her van. I didn't doubt that she'd truly been attempting to read that one chapter all day; her job was demanding, her life was demanding, and she always gave one hundred and ten percent in everything she did.

I dropped my cigarette butt on the asphalt, stomped it out with my white sneaker, picked it up, and threw it in the cigarette butt depository; you had to stomp out your butt before putting it into the genie-bottle-looking holder, or else it would light the other butts inside on fire.

I looked at Maggie sitting in the driver's seat enthralled in her book. I didn't want to disturb her peace, but I thought she'd probably want to read her book in bed, so I knocked on the passenger door to get her attention, waved, and got in the van.

"How did today go, kid?" I loved when Maggie called me 'kid.' She said it in a way that was comforting, and she made me feel like I was still a kid in some ways, which I appreciated. I had always been treated as if I should be a grown up, so Maggie's motherly tone made me feel nurtured.

"Oh, my day was good. Mr. Sawyer thought I was Miss America again, and Mrs. Ricci told me I was the biggest whore there ever was!" We both laughed. I worked on a special care unit for residents with advanced Alzheimer's and Dementia and there was never a dull moment. It was challenging to work on that specific unit, but I had great co-workers, and personally possessed a special talent for caring for their special needs.

"How about you- how was your day?" I asked as she pulled away from the curb and began driving home.

"Oh, the usual. I had a million things to do and then Sonja came and dumped her work on my desk since she had to leave early because her cat got sick." Maggie worked in an accounting office but I was never sure what her actual job was because she seemed to do a bit of everything. Sonja was Maggie's annoying co-worker who regularly took advantage of Maggie's generous nature.

"Isn't Sonja allergic to cats? That's why she said she couldn't come to your Pampered Chef party, because you had cats." I pointed out, hinting that Sonja was a big fat liar.

"Yes, she is." Maggie replied with a pained expression.

"I'm sorry, Maggie. I didn't mean to upset you, I just hate when people take advantage of you. It pisses me off."

"Well, I suppose that's the perfect segue to your letter, Lissy." Maggie said.

"Ok." I became very anxious at the mention of my letter.

"Relax; I'm not mad at you. I help you because I know you're a good kid. You take from me the things you need and nothing more. You, unlike many others, don't take advantage of me. I care about you because I see the good in your heart and I know what you've been through. You don't even have to tell me about it for me to know because I went through the same things as a child. I was adopted and I'm thankful someone cared for me when they didn't have to."

"I understand," she continued, "how difficult it is to trust anyone when the one person you're supposed to be able to trust above anyone in the world lets you down." I knew she was referring to my mother, but I appreciated the fact that she didn't say something nasty about her. No matter what my mother did, I still loved her and didn't like anyone to bash her.

"Thank you," was all I could say in response. Tears were pouring down my face and I was choked up with emotion. I felt overwhelmingly grateful for Maggie's friendship at that moment. What she gave me that day proved invaluable to me for the rest of my life- true compassion and understanding.

Maggie was the one of the only adults in my life to understand that I wasn't someone to be judged or pitied for my tumultuous upbringing. She truly understood that the problems I had adjusting to being a young adult were not a result of my own innate flaws, but a result of my situation. She taught me to be who I am in spite of what I came from, and not to be a product of my environment. With her help, I learned that my past didn't have to define my future, and my choices could bring me great happiness in life if I chose things that would make me happy in life.

Once I realized Maggie's help came from a place of love and genuine compassion, I began to trust others more and forgive myself for all my past mistakes in order to move forward with my life. I stopped judging myself and let go of much of the guilt I held onto for leaving my siblings behind, as I learned that I truly had done what I could in the situation to help them and save them. I also forgave my parents for the hurt they had caused me.

Being out of the house gave me perspective, and though I was hurt that my mother had allowed Ed to put his hands on her children, and create a home of total chaos, I tried to put myself in her shoes as a woman and realized that she was abused too. Even though my mother had failed to meet my most basic human needs as my mother, I forgave her because I realized that, as a person with her own needs that weren't being met, she couldn't be the mother she needed to be for us children.

I don't condone my mother's actions, nor does her own abusive situation justify what she put her children through, but it does explain for me how a mother could allow such things to happen to her children; I feel that I had overlooked or failed to recognize that my mother is was the first victim of Ed's abuse. Giving my forgiveness and having compassion for the person in my life that hurt and betrayed me the most set me free from the anger and sadness that kept me in an endless cycle of misery, trying to understand and fix my past.

Making peace with my past was the best thing I ever could have done for myself; it allowed me to move forward with my life and begin building a new one. I was able to make long-term plans for my future that reflected the things I desired to achieve in life, whereas in the past, my plans had always reflected those of a person in "survival mode"- short-term plans that met my current needs only, with no focus on anything other than just getting through life. I didn't want to just get through life; I wanted to enjoy the journey and truly live.

I gained confidence by setting small goals and achieving them. At the age of eighteen, I finally got my driver's license, which was scary for me because I had always believed driving was a deathly terrifying thing. It wasn't irrational fear that prevented me from learning to drive; I was terrified to do so after an incident with Ed on the farm when I was about ten years old.

We had been planting peppers one weekend until the sun went down and Ed had been drinking beer throughout the entire workday. We weren't very far from our house on the land- probably only about a mile away when a drunken Ed decided it would be fun to "teach" me how to drive his truck home. I was too short to reach the pedals, so he sat right next to me, controlled the pedals, and forced me to control the steering wheel.

I hadn't yet grabbed the steering wheel before he put the truck in drive and pressed hard on the gas, so when we began moving in the direction of a patch of peach trees, I turned the wheel hard in the opposite direction, and we spun nearly three hundred and sixty degrees. Ed laughed hysterically, but I was traumatized. I didn't know how to park the car or get out, so I begged him to stop, but he insisted I drive home so we began again, less crazily that time, but I still swerved back and forth the whole way home. After that day, I had no desire to drive ever again in life, but Maggie convinced me that if I made a new, good memory in a car, it would replace the old bad memory, so I decided to face my fears and at least *try* to drive.

One night after work, a co-worker of mine named Lydia took me out driving on the highway and made it a fun trip, though I was scared to death. We were blasting 50 Cent songs, cruising the speed limit with me at the wheel and her guiding, and encouraging me the entire time. Even though everyone on the road hated me and passed me angrily, I conquered my fear that night, took my driver's test soon after that, and finally got my driver's license. (Thanks Maggie, Lydia, and 50 Cent!)

While living with Maggie, I also began attending an adult high school to obtain my GED. After two classes, my English instructor recommended I discontinue the classes and schedule the GED test since I was already familiar with the material. He felt there was no reason for me to sit through classes if I didn't need to, so I scheduled my GED test, took it, and passed with excellent scores. I felt extremely proud and thankful for everyone who had played a part in my success. As much as I worked hard to face my fears of failure and ineptitude, I couldn't have done it without the help and support of my family of friends.

As all things must certainly do, including the good, my time living with Maggie had to end. I'm sure Maggie would have continued to offer her help to me until the end of time, but unfortunately, she had to end our living arrangement due to the dissolution of her marriage. Saying goodbye to Maggie broke my heart, but I knew our separation was only physical. We promised to keep in touch and visit each other regularly once she was settled from her divorce. Maintaining our relationship wouldn't be difficult; she was planning to stay in the Arbor Falls area since her workplace was nearby.

Because Osenia had moved in with her fiancé to North Jersey near the University he was attending and I worked full-time in Arbor Falls, I had no other option but to move back in with my family. Though it was a dangerous situation to return to that threatened not only my physical safety, but also to undo all of my recent progress, emotionally, and in life, I had to return to the place where all my troubles began.

.

CHAPTER TWENTY-TWO

Returning home after being away for over a year was difficult for me. My normal daily life with Osenia and Maggie was supportive and loving; returning to the misery within the walls of my family home was a crushing disappointment. Not a single thing had changed in my absence except Maddie seemed to have had her soul consumed by dementors and David turned into a nervous wreck, jumping out of his skin at every little noise. Living with my family made me feel as though I were dying just a little more inside with each day that passed.

Armed with a solid plan to stay just long enough to save some more money toward the cost of renting an apartment and buying a car, I put all my efforts into working my full-time job, a part-time job, and taking a few classes at my local community college. I consumed myself with working toward my long-term goals and spent as much time away from the house as possible in hopes I would get the hell out of there as quickly as possible before I was sucked into their dark, twisted world forever.

My thorough plans, which were designed to protect me from the inevitable daily manipulation and verbal abuse I would experience and to make it through the situation as unscathed as possible, weren't foolproof. I had underestimated my mother's ability to create obstacles to my personal success, and had forgotten that she knew exactly how to put me in a vulnerable position.

Maddie and David were hurt I had left them behind when I moved out, but I took great strides to ensure that they knew I thought about them every day and that my intentions were to come back and get them once I was set up. They understood to some degree, but I felt their guardedness with me. All I could do was continue to try my best to get my life together and show them that all my hard work was for them too.

My mother and Ed had come to an extremely violent place with each other and with Maddie and David in my absence. My worst fears had been realized; I left my siblings without protection and they were hurt. The only good thing that came out of that was that Maddie and David had become very close, whereas in the past, they weren't. I had previously protected them from most of the abuse, so they had no real reason to band together. Without me there, they had teamed up and supported each other through their struggles. Although I wished I could have protected them from every ounce of pain they endured, I knew that the resulting closeness in their relationship might not have developed if they hadn't had to be there for each other during hard times.

Though I spent most of my time at work while living with my parents, I did have to be there to sleep, eat, and shower. I had agreed to pay rent while living there, and to buy my own food, so I expected to have few problems with interfering in their lives. Of course, I was wrong. My mother began complaining about needing more financial help, so I agreed to pay more rent. Next, my showers were too long and I was running up the water bill, so I agreed to pay the water bill. Then, even though I was never home, I was running up the electric bill somehow, so I agreed to pay it. Soon enough, I was barely putting any money away in savings for my eventual departure from my parents' home. Even though it was rough, I decided not to allow any of it to sabotage my success. I reminded myself I had a choice and that I could either keep working toward my goal, or allow this obstacle to wreck all the hard work I'd done to get to that point in my life.

My parents increasingly became more hateful toward me as their attempts to sabotage my success failed to throw me off track. They'd sit at the kitchen table insulting me as I walked by, wake me up in the middle of the night when they knew I had a double shift the next day, and limit my showers to ten minutes. If I weren't done in ten minutes, they'd stand outside the door and scream for me to, "get the fuck out."

I can't say their antics didn't hurt me, because I'm human and I'm a sensitive person, and they did, but I didn't really care what they thought of me. Having had the chance to see what life was like outside of an abusive situation; I pitied them and felt that their opinions of me had no weight in my self-esteem anymore. While sure, they could hurt me, I wasn't going to allow them to take me down entirely.

The strength I attempted to maintain and display was viewed as snobbery by my parents; they took my attitude as that of a person who thinks they're superior to others.

Because of their opinion that I was insulting them by acting as if they were beneath me, they decided I needed to be knocked down a few notches and put in my place, so the beatings I'd endured growing up began again.

Once the physical abuse resumed, I knew my exit plan needed to be adjusted so I could leave sooner than originally planned. Since buying freedom from abuse hadn't worked to my advantage, I decided to stop paying my mother's extra bills and only paid the agreed-upon rent so I could hoard the money to leave for good, which is all I truly wished for, more than anything in the whole entire world. I didn't desire riches or fame; all I wanted was to be free to live my life without the pain of abuse. Little did I know, I would get my wish much sooner than I originally thought.

*   *   *   *   *

As I tiptoe through the upstairs hall of our old farmhouse, I silently pray I don't wake my stepfather. A few steps down the cold hardwood floor I stop in front of my little brother's room when I see a faint trace of light. When I peek my head in, I see that he has built a small fort in the corner of his room made solely from his SpongeBob Squarepants comforter and many cleverly placed thumbtacks. Outside his fort, he has arranged his Army Man action figures in a straight line protecting the small entrance.

"What are you doing, David?" I whisper to him from the doorway. Poking his head through the entrance of the fort, he shines his flashlight directly into my eyes, momentarily blinding me. He looks at me with his big brown eyes, and begins opening his mouth to speak.

Instead, he stops mid-sentence and puts his head down.

"What's wrong?" I ask, trying to blink away the white dots now floating across my vision.

"Nothing," he replies. I know that's not the truth.

I walk over to him and sit down on the floor outside of his fort. "You can tell me if something's wrong, David. I'm here if you need to talk."

"I want to go live with Mom-mom."

I'd like to go live with Mom-mom too, I think to myself.

"I know you love being at Mom-mom's house, and you will be there tomorrow after school. Go to sleep. The sooner you go to sleep, the sooner you'll be there." He smiles slightly, only partially consoled, and lays his head down on his pillow.

"Yes, I'm going to Mom-mom's house tomorrow, and I'm never coming back here," he says with anger and sadness in his voice.

I carefully reach inside the fort and lift my hand, gently brushing his eyelids closed with my fingertips as I had done nearly every night when he was an infant. He would fall asleep so easily that way in his bassinette; I hoped it would have the same effect this night. He snuggles further down into the heap of fluffy blankets inside his fort and prepares for sleep. I back out of his protective cave slowly and carefully, as not to tear it down or disturb the Army Men standing at attention outside, and leave him to his dream world.

As I pull his bedroom door closed as softly and with as little noise as possible, I hear the faint sound of the wooden floor creaking down the hall. With my hand still holding on to the door handle, I hold my breath to listen for the source of the sound, barely able hear anything over the pounding of my own heart beating madly out of my chest.

I stand still as a statue feeling adrenaline racing through me, my knuckles white from the tight grip I wasn't aware I had on the doorknob. My body trembling and frozen with fear, I stand there waiting and listening. I hear someone getting out of bed.

Oh, shit. I should've just gone to bed and minded my own damned business.

I can feel my heart leaping into my throat and my stomach churn as my dinner does somersaults inside; I have woken my parents, and for this, I will surely pay.

"What are you doing, Lissy?" My mother asks in a tone that implies I'm up to no good. When she flips on the hallway light, I squint my eyes from the sudden brightness. I see her standing barefoot at the end of the hall in her fuchsia-colored robe, one hand puffing on a cigarette, and the other placed casually on her hip.

"I was just checking on David, that's all." I said, voice wavering from fear. I couldn't stop my body from shaking. I knew Ed would be out in a moment to take care of me.

"Oh ok, so you felt it necessary to wake the whole house up to do so? You're a selfish little bitch, Lissy. Ed will handle you. I wash my hands of you; you leave this house for one year and think you're better than everyone here, don't you?" She asks menacingly.

"No, I never said that," I deny.

"You and Maggie and her holier-than-thou attitude are

going to band together and save the world, huh? Do you think Maggie really gives two shits about you? She only had you there because she's one of those people who just love to fix people so she can feel better about her shitty life; her actions are self-serving and you're too stupid to see it. Nobody likes you, Lissy. You're a fake and a phony, and you can't just move to a new house and pretend you're not shit because you are. No matter where you are in this world, you'll always be the loser slut who thinks the world revolves around her."

Behind her, Ed appears looking drunk and angry. As he starts toward me, I back away, hands up in defense.

"I'm sorry I woke you up, Ed. I didn't mean to. I was just checking on David and he was having trouble sleeping. I didn't mean-"a hard hit to my temple sends me falling to the floor.

Before I can scream or act, a barrage of hits to my face and torso keep me stunned and silent. It's all happening so fast, it's as if I'm in a terrible dream unable to wake myself up. The first few hits hurt terribly on impact, but after repeated punches, I feel numb and faint as my head is thrown left and right from the force of the blows. I taste the saltiness of blood in my mouth and feel the warm wetness of it trickling down from my cheek into my ear. I lie there unable to defend myself and consciously fear I may actually die this time. As the blows continue, I feel less and less able to maintain awareness and close my eyes to welcome the darkness of unconsciousness as a warm puddle of urine spreads underneath me out of my control.

*　　*　　*　　*　　*

"Please, Lissy, wake up! Oh my God! Please wake up!" I awake from my blackout to Maddie screaming and crying on top of me. She's shaking me hard and crying hysterically.

I wonder how long I was out. I think to myself, dazed.

"Oh, God, Lissy. Look what he did to your face! They fucking did this shit to you, I fucking hate them!" Hearing Maddie's hysterical screams break my heart and seeing her cry at the top of her lungs at the sight of me makes me scared to look in the mirror.

"Maddie, I'm ok, I promise." From the sound of that sentence, I can tell my lip is blown up like a balloon. I can't see very well, but I can't tell if it's because I'm not wearing my contacts, or because my eyes are swollen shut. I'm afraid to look. My entire face feels like it's on fire and my neck hurts terribly. Lifting my sore arm to touch my hand to my head, I touch a tender lump on my forehead and immediately pull my hand away from the stinging pain. I look at my hand and notice blood streaked on my fingers.

"I heard the whole thing. Oh my God, it was horrible. Lissy, you're very badly hurt," Maddie informs me in barely comprehensible sobs. "I hate them for this. I'm going to kill them." Her tears are pouring down her cheeks and I cannot stand to see her so upset.

"Maddie, can you help me up so I can get cleaned up please? Don't worry, I am definitely going to be ok, I guarantee it." To be honest, I'm not sure whether I'm going to be ok or not, I've certainly suffered a head injury, but I'm conscious, so that's a plus, but my whole body feels like I've been hit by a truck and I can't sit up on my own. I'm not sure if I have broken ribs or what, but I'm in the worst pain of my life.

"Yes, I can help you," she says, sniveling. "I can't believe they did this to you. They are evil and twisted, Lissy!"

"Yes, they definitely are, now just put one arm under me, around my shoulders, and the other arm under my legs where my knees are and just push me in an upright sitting position, ok?" I instruct.

"Ok." Maddie looks scared to death to hurt me more by moving me. "Do you think we should call 9-1-1?"

"No, please don't call them. I really don't want to spend the night in the hospital. They ask too many questions and I don't want family services involved. I don't have the resources yet to get custody of David and they will place him in foster care. No, please. I'd rather just wait until I have enough money saved to establish myself and then get custody of David. I'm almost there financially, so please, please do NOT call 9-1-1."

"I won't." She promises as she sits me upright.

I groan in response to the pain in the lower right part of my abdomen. I'm no doctor, but something is seriously wrong there. Though I feel dizzy and nauseous sitting up, I want to stand up and head to the bathroom. Instead of doing so, I decide to sit there a little while longer and try to regain some composure.

"Where are Mommy and Ed?" I ask, curious as to where they are while we're in the upstairs hallway making all this noise.

"They're downstairs in the kitchen having a grand old time; laughing and drinking coffee. I fucking hate them,

Lissy! They don't deserve to live."

"I hate them too, but really, they are the miserable ones down there feeding off my pain. Once no children are in the home, they'll turn on each other. Guess who will be laughing then? They're idiots. I could care less what either of them thinks of me. Ed can beat me every single day just like he did today, but I will never become like them. They're disgusting excuses for human beings."

Maddie stands leaning against the wall looking through me, with red, tear-stained cheeks, deep in thought.

"Hey Mad, can you run me a hot bath please?" I ask, disrupting her thoughts.

"Sure. You want to just sit here a minute?"

"Yeah, I'm still pretty dizzy, so I'm just going to wait a few more minutes before I try to stand up."

"Ok, I'll run a bath for you, just sit there. Do you need anything else in the meantime?"

"Yes, new parents, and a cold Pepsi. Thanks, waitress." I joke.

Rolling her teary eyes, Maddie says, "Only you are twisted enough to make a joke in this kind of situation." She smiles sadly, but I know my joke lightened the mood at least a little bit. "I can get you a Pepsi, but non-psychotic parents are on backorder, so you'll have to wait a long time for them to come in."

"Mad! You made a funny! I'm so proud of you! With your black hair and undead cronies, I'd thought you'd joined the dark side for good!" I chuckle teasingly as she attempts to hide her smile.

"Whatever, shut up and get in this tub," she points to the almost-full tub, "before I get my zombie friends to come over and throw you in. Ha!"

"Two in a row, good job! 'It's alive!'" I say dramatically, as I hold onto the wall to stand up. Straightening myself out, I feel able to try to walk from the hallway into the bathroom to get in the tub. After a few careful steps, I feel confident that I'm balanced enough to make it to the tub by myself and walk over to sit on the side of it.

"Whatever, Lissy. Walking the way you just did, you're more like Frankenstein than I am." Laughing, she throws a washcloth in my face and sets a towel on the sink for me.

"Yeah, yeah. Come check on me in like twenty minutes, ok?"

"Yes, my queen," she says sarcastically as she shuts the door behind her.

After undressing, I ease into the tub and let the hot water soothe the ache in my muscles. I try my hardest not to pay attention to the fact that my bathwater is turning red or to think about what just happened because I don't want to be stuck in the pain and drama this abuse causes me. There's only one way to get through this and eventually free from it forever, and that's to endure it while I'm here and not allow these situations to stop me from accomplishing what I need to be doing to get out of here.

I dip my washcloth into the hot water and lay it on my face so it covers it. I sit for a moment with it on my face like that until it feels dry, but when I take it away, I see the blood, and it scares me. I can't scrub my face because it hurts too badly, so I just dip the washcloth in the water and wring it out over my face, hoping most of it will wash away with repeated splashes of water. I'm trying hard to maintain my composure and not get upset, but the more my bathwater reddens in color, the more I fear what the damage looks like.

I sit in the tub until the water gets cold, then drain the bloody water and turn on the shower. I scrub my body clean, gently wash my hair, trying not to touch the swollen lumps in my head, and let the water rain down on my sore face. When I finally get out, I wrap my towel around my aching body and prepare myself emotionally for the sight I'm about to see in the mirror.

I step in front of the white porcelain sink and stare at the brushed metal finished knobs. Placing my hands on either side of the sink, I brace myself for what I'm about to see. When I look up, I see a face I don't recognize. The girl in the mirror has both eyes swollen almost completely shut, one with a broken blood vessel covering the entire white part of the eye, and the other with a small red dot to the left side of the iris. She also has several large knots on her face, one on her upper-right forehead, one on her left side of her head, partially hidden by her hairline, and one on her lower cheek that meets with her swollen, busted lower lip. I know the girl in the mirror is me, but surveying the disfigured face in front of me has me in disbelief.

It's difficult to explain in words how it feels to truly look at yourself in the mirror, both literally and figuratively, and realize that you've allowed yourself to be put in a situation you know is a true threat to your well-being. I suppose that when I came back home to a physically abusive situation, I believed the violence would only reach a certain limit; one I was familiar with and could deal with. Seeing the severity of the injuries to my battered face and body was alarming and made me realize that there's no such thing as a limit in violence. Death could occur as a result of a beating just as easily as a broken bone. Battered women die all the time at the hands of their abusers. Did I think I was immune to this fact?

The realization that I could be dead right now hit me with cold, hard, reality; I can't stay here anymore and neither can my siblings. Our lives are truly in danger and I'm not being dramatic. Though I had feared our deaths in the past, part of me didn't truly believe it would ever go that far. Now, considering my recent loss of consciousness and current physical state, I finally acknowledge that it will go that far, intentionally or otherwise, and in order to preserve the lives of my siblings, as well as my own, I have to leave this house. I have to leave now, not in six months, or three.

The time is now.

EPILOGUE

I'd love to be able to say that after I took my siblings and left my parents' house that night that the three of us lived happily ever after, but this is real life and reality is no fairy tale.

The night we left, we stayed at Mom-mom's house, and my grandparents finally realized that Ed had truly been abusing us and not simply disciplining us. I felt some sort of vindication at last, having my grandparents believe me, but at the same time, let down that my siblings and I had to endure so much pain because they didn't believe us sooner.

My grandparents apologized repeatedly for not knowing, and I forgave them. They came from a generation where physical discipline was normal, and as my mother had presented Ed's punishments as discipline and had gone to much effort to hide obvious injuries, my grandparents had no way to truly know who to believe, so I understood. The fact that I finally had their understanding and support was what mattered most to me.

I ended up filing a police report for the first time,

documenting the abuse that had occurred over the years since Ed had entered our lives. Finally spilling my secrets to the police was cathartic and therapeutic, though painful and difficult. They took pictures of all my injuries and told me they would handle all the legal matters. For some reason, I personally did not want to press charges. I just wanted to move on with my life and not have any strings attached to my old life. Still, they prosecuted Ed and my mother on their own; I didn't have to participate.

Maddie and David stayed with my grandparents for a few weeks while my friend Jessa's mother allowed me to stay with them so I could save several more paychecks for my move. A few weeks later, I had enough cash to secure a one-bedroom apartment in a town far enough away from Arbor Falls to avoid my parents, but close enough to my workplace and Mom-mom and Pop-pop's house so that I could keep my current jobs and David could continue going to my grandparents' house after school. I also got a car with no down payment, thanks to my good credit, which allowed us to get around. Maddie had quit high school and begun working at a fast food restaurant while I had been living with Maggie, so the location we chose was ideal for her as well.

Living on our own proved difficult; we were all still hurting from the life we had led together with our parents and some of that hurt ended up causing issues in our relationships with each other and eventually, the three of us went our separate ways.

David was the first to go; he missed his parents greatly soon after our move, and wanted to go back home, a request I couldn't technically refuse, but tried my best to persuade him out of. Despite my best efforts, David went back to live with my parents after a short time living with Maddie and me. I'm happy to say that neither of my parents ever laid a hand on him when he went back, but sadly, the emotional abuse never ended. David, in his desperation and loneliness, got involved in a street gang and began doing drugs. By the time he was fourteen years old, David was too far gone for me to reach. Though he struggles with addiction and the pain caused by our childhood, David and I remain close.

Maddie stayed with me the longest and was an extremely hard worker at her fast food job. We became very close friends while living together, and I came to love her more than I ever had before watching her try so hard to live a normal life, but not quite succeeding. The damage done to Maddie resulting from the abuse we endured was great. She struggled with Post-Traumatic Stress Disorder, Depression, and Panic Disorder and had a terrible time trying to overcome her emotional obstacles without professional help while maintaining a full time job and trying to have a new life free from abuse.

Freedom was a scary thing for Maddie. She didn't quite know what to do with her life when she wasn't constantly consumed by negativity. She was always waiting for the next bad thing to happen, anticipating the worst, and confused when nothing bad happened. In addition, she became very angry that she'd been robbed of her happiness for so many years and became very angry with our parents and the world.

After becoming overwhelmed with anger and guilt, Maddie moved in with Mom-mom and Pop-pop. Maddie has fallen down in life so many times since we left that night, but the one thing I admire about her the most is that she always, without fail, gets back up and fights vigorously. She may have suffered the most because of what we went through in that house, but she's also the one who has remained the most beautiful inside. Maddie's heart is one made of pure gold.

As for my parents, I had been correct in my prediction that they would turn on each other once no children were in the home. They had had a brief period of the honeymoon phase after I reported them to the police; I suppose standing together against my allegations of abuse made them feel a strong sense of togetherness. However, after Ed was charged and got a mild slap on the wrist and no jail time, things went downhill in their relationship, not just because of the absence of children, but because they were faced with the reality that the problems in the home existed without us.

It's hard for me to imagine that my parents could have truly believed we, the children, were the cause of their misery and the reason they acted as they did, but as I've learned throughout my years in recovery from abuse, denial is a strong psychological defense mechanism. They had to believe we were the problem; if they didn't, they'd be forced to take blame for their own unhappiness, a reality too undesirable to be acceptable. Once faced with this reality, they turned on each other. Ed disappeared for days on end and my mother would drive around town for hours looking for him. Ed became consumed with drinking all day every day, and my mother became consumed with Ed.

Then, something happened that changed the game between them; my mother suffered a stroke, and then was diagnosed with late stage breast cancer. Once she was no longer able to work, drive, chase him around, or perform her wifely duties, Ed wanted no part of their marriage any longer. Once my mother was in a vulnerable, needy position and could no longer provide Ed the things he needed her for, he found himself a younger woman and left my mother with absolutely nothing.

He didn't tell any of us he was leaving, nor did he make any plans for the care of my mother or his son. We found out he was leaving when the sheriff showed up at my family home and informed my mother that she had three days to move out, a shocking order Ed had known about but decided to keep to himself; he had stopped paying the mortgage entirely at some point, yet never asked for help or told any of us.

Ed left my mother ill, penniless, and homeless, and despite all the times our mother had chosen Ed over us, Maddie and I stepped in to clean up his mess. Maddie and David moved in with our mother after Ed left to help her get around and to assist with finances. Though I live apart from them, I do what I can financially and otherwise to help them. It hasn't been easy, as my mother isn't the best patient or mother in the world, but considering her past and all the suffering she went through being with Ed, I understand her emotional state and I still love my mother despite what she put us all through.

None of us speaks to Ed, except for David, since Ed is his father, but Ed doesn't really care to have much to do with David. Although I do forgive Ed for the ways he hurt me as a child, I find it difficult to forgive him for the ways he neglects his son now, and the way he left our ill mother, leaving behind such a rough existence for all of us. Still, we're all better off without him in our lives. Knowing that none of us has to endure his abuse any longer is comforting.

As for me, I've fallen down a number of times in life since I left the house where I was broken. Like Maddie, I always get up and try again, press on, and try my damnedest to learn from my mistakes, but it certainly takes me longer than Maddie to get myself back up after a huge fall. I suffer from the side effects of abuse in many ways, but the most debilitating is my struggle with Panic Disorder, Social Anxiety Disorder, Depression, Agoraphobia, and self-doubt.

My panic attacks began when I was roughly sixteen years old, but were not a re-occurring problem until I lived alone in the apartment I had shared with Maddie and David. I'm not sure why they began, but once they started, they came unannounced and unwelcomed at the most inopportune moments. Because of my lack of faith in the mental health system, I did not seek professional help and suffered in silence with chronic panic attacks that quickly turned me into an agoraphobic hermit, which in turn triggered a serious Obsessive-Compulsive Disorder episode. Because of my shame and embarrassment of my secret ailments, I also developed a phobia of social situations.

I suffered many years in silence by avoiding things that triggered panic attacks. Because of my avoidance behavior, my world became very small, but I was creative and somehow made it work. I went to college online from home and ended up working from home when I could, but could not work a traditional job, travel, shop, work, or drive outside of my "safe zone."

Some people think Agoraphobia means you can't leave the house, and for many, it often does, but in the world of the panic-ridden, Agoraphobics can also venture out to different places where they feel safe, and the fear of being in places deemed unsafe to the sufferer is also considered Agoraphobia.

I met my husband when I was twenty-two in one of my "safe places." He was a Staff Sergeant in the United States Air Force and one of the most handsome guys I had ever met, as well as kind, and one of the only men in my life to ever give me proper respect. My husband believed in me from the start; he was and still is my greatest supporter in life, and though he doesn't always understand the things I've gone through in my childhood, he tries his hardest to work with me through my trust issues and my neurotic, anxious ways. I give him much credit for all the ways he works hard to put all the broken pieces of me back together and I will always and forever love him for that.

My husband and I married after six years of him convincing me that marriage could indeed be a good thing, despite what I believed to be true based on my parents' marriage. We were married in October of 2011 in a beautiful ceremony that included my "family of friends." Mr. Hiller, my high school music teacher, gave me away, while my oldest friend Sophie was my Maid of Honor. Osenia, who had been there for me through so much, served as my Matron of Honor. Jessa was one of my bridesmaids, as was Maddie, who probably shouldn't have been anywhere near the open bar during the reception. In attendance, of course, was Maggie, my other mother, along with everyone who had been a huge part of helping me overcome my rocky childhood.

Maddie and I just celebrated our thirtieth birthday and David is now twenty years old. My mother's health is poor, but she can talk and write normally now, and the four of us have been working together repairing our relationship as a family. Though we've all had pieces of us taken away by the pain we've suffered, we try every day to move forward and live our lives happily, healthily, and fully; something we'll surely be working toward for many years to come.

ACKNOWLEDGEMENTS

There are several people I want to thank who have made a huge impact in my life and in the making of this book, and in order to maintain my own anonymity and that of the people represented in this book, this list is in random order and includes people not depicted in this memoir.

Special thanks to:

My husband JT, Mommy Dearest with her Bucary, Ethel, Corby, My Mom-mom and Pop-pop, T-bot and Mama Kathy, Debbi-mom & J-Rad, Dr. & Mrs. C, TT & Boogie, DTM & family, Jazzyface & Mamacita, Gigi, Q, & the T family from fifth street, La, "The Boys," including Randy, despite the wedding incident, my crazy in-laws, my beautiful step-daughter, Justin (WB), AJW, and last, but not least, Daisey Mae, Cookie, Chickie, Janet, "All the cats," and Nika & Pick-L.

I'd also like to thank all my family members, especially "Uncle Nick & Aunt Roxie," "Annabelle," Aurora's mom, Uncle Bobbles & Aunt Li (Earl still loves you), Aunt S, and all of my crazy, yet fabulous, cousins.

I love you all and am so grateful for your presence in my life- past, present, and future.

-*Adriana Bellini*

INFORMATION

If you or someone you know is suffering from child abuse, and you live in the U.S.A. or Canada, please call *"The Childhelp National Child Abuse Hotline* **1-800-4-A-CHILD (1-800-422-4453)"** which "is dedicated to the prevention of child abuse."

"Serving the United States, its territories, and Canada, the Hotline is staffed **24 hours a day, 7 days a week** with professional crisis counselors who, through interpreters, can provide assistance in 170 languages. The Hotline offers crisis intervention, information, literature, and referrals to thousands of emergency, social service, and support resources. **All calls are anonymous and confidential."** (www.childhelp.org, 2013)*

*"National Child Abuse Hotline." *Prevention and Treatment of Child Abuse*. N.p., 2013. Web. 19 July 2013.

ADRIANA BELLINI

ABOUT THE AUTHOR

Adriana Bellini is an American author, born and raised in a small town in New Jersey just outside of Philadelphia. An animal lover who frequently rescues feral cats, she enjoys reading, writing, painting, singing, and cooking with her husband, a United States Air Force Staff Sergeant.

A veteran in the nursing field and current student of psychology, Adriana draws from her experiences in her career field and education background to create her works.

Adriana is currently living in Edgewater Park, New Jersey with her husband and their three cats while working on her next novel.

31372537R00109

Made in the USA
Lexington, KY
09 April 2014